A Spark of the Divine

A Soul's Journey
Through Time, Space and Beyond

A Spark
of the Divine

A Soul's Journey
Through Time, Space and Beyond

Nancy Van Domelen

Shining Mountain Publishing

Shining Mountain Publishing
www.shiningmountain.net
info@shiningmountain.net

Ordering Information:
Special discounts are available on quantity purchases.
For further information, contact the publisher at the address above.

Cover art by Marika Popovits
Cover and interior design by Cathy Bowman
Printed and bound in the United States of America by Color House Graphics

ISBN: 978-0-9716106-2-0
Library of Congress Control Number: 2011902865

First Edition

10   9   8   7   6   5   4   3   2   1

I dedicate this book
to the incarnating souls on Earth
who are expanding their spiritual consciousness.
During this great awakening, many are becoming aware
that they possess a soul essence at the core of their being.
This knowledge will assist humanity in taking
the next step towards a new and better world.

TABLE OF CONTENTS

ACKNOWLEDGEMENTS

Different people have come into my life to assist in many ways during the years I have been receiving ongoing messages from the realm of spirit. I want to express my love and appreciation to all who have walked along with me, especially the following:

Rebecca VanDenBerghe, whose editing skills always showed ongoing respect for the transmissions while maintaining their clarity and integrity.

Marika Popovits, whose art work on the cover beautifully symbolizes the soul essence described in this book. Marika's ability to express the reality of spiritual realms through her paintings is a gift to us all.

Jackie Karsky, a sister in spirit, who has been involved in every part of this spiritual journey for the past five years. Her contribution has been invaluable.

Puja Parsons, who energetically grounded every transmission from the realm of spirit included in this book. I am grateful for her involvement.

Elizabeth Hare, who provided researching skills and most significantly encouragement at the outset of the publishing work on this book.

Marianne Green, Margaret Gilfoyle, Constance Shambo, John Audette, Marika Popovits, Jackie Karsky, Elizabeth Hare and Shelley Burke who reviewed the completed manuscript with such love and respect. Their contribution was an essential part of the overall effort.

Cathy Bowman and Color House Graphics for their role in bringing the information from spirit into print.

My husband, Peter, for his ongoing support at every level of this endeavor. His involvement has been a blessing.

My family, which is a source of love and joy for me. The richness of these relationships has provided a framework for my work down through the years.

INTRODUCTION

As I reflect upon all that has transpired since I began receiving transmissions from the realm of spirit in the early 1980's, I cannot help but recognize the vast change this process has effected in me. The messages from spirit began several years after the death of my son in 1979 in the form of letters from him. My love for him was a catalyst impelling me to pursue something well beyond my comprehension at the time.

For many years, my journey was private and highly personal. On a continuous basis, I received transmissions in the form of letters from the realm of spirit. At first, the contacts were from my son who had died. Eventually these contacts came from a group of souls who called themselves the Lightbringers. Their message was then expanded into the publication of two books, *Dreaming a New World* and *The Higher Dimensions: Our Next Home*.

Down through the years, my journey has been one of discovery and transformation. When I began the process of personal journaling in the early 1980s, I was tentative and questioning, always keeping my contact with the realm of spirit as a separate part of my life. It was a segment complete unto itself that had little impact on the mundane aspects of my daily existence.

Gradually, however, the thoughts, ideas and teachings from spirit began to permeate my very being. I found that my views of the world and the people about me were transformed gradually but inexorably. The relationships in my life started to change and become more harmonious. My physical health improved, and life seemed more serene, even when stressful events occurred.

Continually working with a group soul in another dimension became as natural as visiting with human friends, even though I never was able to see my spiritual companions. Their messages were wise, loving, and directly applicable to many issues I was facing at the time. In summary, I slowly found myself viewing life from a new and more profound perspective, a process that imprinted me in many ways.

I now offer a third book of messages from the realm of spirit, quite different from the first two. This new book moves more deeply into the realm of universal and multidimensional consciousness, giving a comprehensive presentation of the soul's journey through time, space and beyond. All three books are encoded with a vibrational force field as significant as the content within. For many readers, a mental and spiritual expansion occurs as they connect with the energy infused in these works.

The vibrational qualities emanating from the spiritual source of each book had very definable characteristics. The transmissions for *Dreaming a New World* seemed loving, nurturing, poetic and almost feminine in nature. *The Higher Dimensions: Our Next Home* had a more urgent masculine quality permeating the messages found within.

The group soul bringing information for this third book, however, possessed a spiritual essence unlike any I had encountered in my twenty-five years of receiving. I will do the best to describe it, even though words cannot begin to give an accurate depiction. The source of these transmissions felt like pure will and possessed a powerful mind force that was direct and penetrating. In addition, the source of the information reflected a vibratory field that seemed almost crystalline in nature.

Although many profound ideas were presented with a minimum of words, they resonated with a power that I felt at the core of my being. I was told by my source that, even though the brain would be processing the verbal content, the spiritual power within would be received and processed by the heart. Finally, meditation was urged as the pathway to the soul and to the space between thoughts that holds the essence of God.

So it is that I offer with great humility the transmissions I received from the realm of spirit. It is said often in this book that we must access the soul, which is our birthright, in order to move forward spiritually. Also, it is time for the people of Earth to realize they are sparks of divine energy sent out from the Creator. The primary purpose in life for all souls is to grow in love and wisdom, ultimately returning to the source from which they came. May this book assist and uplift you on your journey!

Nancy Van Domelen
2011

CHAPTER 1

Let Us Continue

We welcome you, our dear friends, as we begin this third book, formed from a partnership between the realm of spirit and the plane of matter. In our first book, *Dreaming a New World*, we offered a spiritual perspective concerning many personal issues that are part of the human condition. The second book, *The Higher Dimensions: Our Next Home,* was planetary in scope, focusing on Earth's initiation into higher consciousness, the polarity of conflict throughout the globe, and humanity's entrance into the fourth dimension of time.

We now ask that you join us again as we continue with this third book, which will present a universal spiritual theme. It will deal primarily with the nature of the soul and its journey throughout the many realms of time, space and beyond until it ultimately returns to the Source of All That Is. We bring this information to those living on Earth so they can realize that they possess an essence of the Creator guiding and sustaining them at all levels.

This book contains light-encoded vibratory waves of information about the realm of spirit and the journey all souls are taking on the way to reunion with the Divine Creator. This journey can be arduous or filled with joy, depending on the life lessons being experienced at the time. Every soul enters into many different archetypal life conditions in order to provide Source with what has been manifested in the world of matter.

We, as a group soul, have been given the responsibility for beaming information onto Earth that will increase the knowledge base of those living in the third dimension. It is time for you to open your eyes, lift your heads and connect with the greater world in which you live. You reside within a galaxy that is teeming with a multiplicity of diverse life forms, and your galaxy is only one of many occupying the spaces of your universe.

The Power Source of Creation

All existence has, at its core, a spiritual essence transmitted from the Divine Creator. Incorporate this knowledge into the picture of who you are and why you exist. Without this awareness, your focus is wholly material and lacking broader comprehension. It is as if you have been living in a closed box set in a lush and beautiful setting surrounding you, one that you cannot see.

All life emerges from the Mind of God as Idea. It then progresses to the densest level, where it manifests in form. This is the pattern for all the universes of the Creator. Each thought, word or action emanates from this divine flow of energy, permeating everything that exists. Pure Idea emitted from the Mind of God is the ultimate source for life, no matter how diverse.

The children of Earth live in the intense vibratory matrix of the third dimension, which was created purely for the purpose of irradiating dense matter with the light-filled rays of spirit. The ultimate aim of this union is to bring two different kinds of creation together in a unified field of great power and beauty.

In order to accomplish this universal task, opposing forces join in a dance of cosmic proportions. It is this dance of duality that forms the background for all that exists. We ask our readers to attune to the rhythm of this great energy field. Its beat permeates every aspect of life, no matter how diverse.

When you begin to feel the vibration of the Primal Source, you have reached a level of sensitivity that will move you multidimensionally to other areas of your universe. All patterns of light and sound exist in beautiful waves throughout time and space. As the physical molecules of your human bodies become illuminated with the spiritual essence of the Creator, you will be able to experience the harmony of the spheres.

Whether or not you are aware of it, this throbbing pulsation provides the power source for every aspect of creation. Without it there would be no life anywhere. As each person living on Earth grows in sensitivity, more light will be brought into his or her energy field. The ability to become aware of and attune to this primal rhythm of life will increase to the point where anyone will be able to draw upon this energy source solely through the power of intent.

Remembering Who You Are

It is now time for the inhabitants of Earth to remember that they possess a spiritual essence that infuses the life force in their bodies and generates the energetic matrix for their human experience. In earliest times, all those living on your planet knew that they possessed, at their core, the spiritual energy of the Creator. They knew also that they had come into being in order to provide their Source with the awareness of what it was to experience life at various levels of existence.

In recent decades, science has focused upon how the many universes of life originated. The currently accepted explanation is the Big Bang Theory, which postulates the emergence of life as an explosion of matter radiating out from a central energy field of great power. And there is much truth in this theory. What has not been addressed is the nature of this unknown energy field or its origin.

Science has described the process of creation without offering an explanation concerning the force generating the Big Bang. The focus of study has been on what transpired after the explosion occurred. If the main emphasis had been on exploring what kind of energy field would be powerful enough to bring a wide variety of life into being, it would be possible to recognize the true nature of the Source of All Life.

Material creation emanates from a central vortex of condensed mind force. This mind force embodies the divine essence of will, love, wisdom and intelligence. As people pray to a Higher Power, whatever their religious faith or spiritual inclination, this is basically what they are connecting to, even though they may not be aware of it. When people invoke a divinity they visualize in human form, they actually are accessing only one of the many attributes of God.

We speak of this concept now because the twenty-first century is the time when incarnating souls on the Earth plane will be coming back to the knowledge they had in the earliest days on the planet. They will begin to see that they were created to take a great journey of exploration and to experience all that God had manifested in the dimensions of time, space and beyond. After doing so, they will finally merge into union with the Creator, as fully realized and enlightened beings, children of the God Force.

Our books provide a gentle entry into this concept of multidimensional consciousness. They are created to reach people through their easily acceptable spiritual content. The vast body of humanity is expanding its current intellectual boundaries and exploring ideas that seemed beyond comprehension just a short while ago.

We offer love and support to this group of incarnating souls as they start to open the doorway into higher spiritual awareness. The ideas presented in these books are meant to slowly expand comprehension through a process that resembles remembering. Very often the reader will experience a sense of familiarity with the material, making acceptance much easier.

At the same time, the reader is being impulsed with higher vibrational energy waves that help dissolve old crystallized thought patterns, providing space for new beliefs to enter the mental processes and take hold. When one is stretched too far beyond a comfort level, it is difficult to increase consciousness. We are opening the door with love and gentle encouragement. By so doing, we provide either a brief look or an actual step through to the other side, whatever is desired.

Our information has within it a heart resonance calibration. Certain information from spirit currently is aimed at bringing about a shift in mental outlook—something sorely needed at this time. Other information, such as ours, is designed to open the heart chakra so that light and love can be beamed onto the planet with ever-increasing intensity. Both purposes have equal validity and importance in the spiritual scheme of things, because the joining of mind and heart will usher in a New World that is waiting to come forth.

Now we would like to speak about the presentation of the content of this book. The reader will find certain words, phrases and basic themes appearing more than once. The material is assembled in this manner to give the reader a sense of the fourth dimension of time, where everything occurs simultaneously and sometimes repetitively. So when you come upon certain ideas and expressions you have read before in the book, know that they are being repeated for emphasis because they are important.

Repetition is an integral part of the learning process. All life moves in a circular fashion, coming back to the same place it has revolved past. This circle exists, however, within the greater form of a spiral, which lifts every recurrence up to a slightly higher level of expression. This explains why experience is such a valuable teacher. True wisdom is gained through the repetition of an idea or situation until comprehension and mastery are reached.

Creativity—A New Concept for Living

The inhabitants of your planet are now ready to connect with the reality of their world, as well as the many different dimensions coexisting throughout time and space. They must start to realize that they are spiritual beings encased in a physical body, which provides the opportunity of living in one of the most intense levels of the Creator's world—that of the third dimension.

We ask that you reconnect with the lost knowledge regarding who and what you really are. You are units of the Supreme Being sent forth to travel throughout time and space into many seemingly strange and unfamiliar realms in order to learn about the many aspects of the God Force on a personal level.

At the outset of creation in your current universe, the Primal Being emitted a great and powerful breath, which coalesced into a wide variety of worlds. This act was the ultimate expression of creativity and set the tone for emerging life everywhere. Because creativity was the primary energy released, it constitutes the foundational quality of all life, whatever its variety or form.

The need to create is the basis for everything that exists. We bring this information now to acquaint you with your primary purpose for living. If people on Earth were asked to identify the most important thing they could do in a lifetime, the rare individual would say "to create." The usual response would be a mundane accomplishment fulfilled on the three-dimensional level.

It is true that many achievements involve creative effort, but they generally are viewed in regard to the physical results they provide. What we are speaking about here is the honoring of every action because it reflects the creative essence of the God Force and conveys to all elements of life the highest spiritual expression possible. The primary purpose of creativity is to bring love and joy, not to produce concrete results, even though results may be a desired outcome.

When an incarnating soul focuses on the innate desire to create and applies it to every aspect of life, existence is raised to a higher level of spiritual development. Joy is found in the simplest of acts, and life starts to unfold in a beautiful, harmonious rhythm, pulsating in union with the Source of All That Is. Creation is seen then as the ultimate act of love and a reflection of the God Force itself.

CHAPTER 2

Plan of the Creator

The inhabitants of Earth are moving into a pivotal time in their evolutionary growth. Your planet is being bombarded with a concentration of subatomic particles emanating from the center of your galaxy. Approximately every 12,000 years, your solar system moves into a place in the galaxy where it receives potent and direct waves of energy, which imprint every area of the globe.

The greatest source of creativity is always found at the center of every solar system, galaxy and universe. From this point, the God Force radiates powerful waves of energy that form the cornerstone for life throughout all the realms of time and space. Universal laws regulate these emissions, creating evolutionary cycles, which provide the matrix for soul development. This is the foundation for everything that lives in your world.

The single most important realization one can come to is the certainty that human existence follows a steady evolutionary path through diverse realms, as you learn how to live in all the dimensions of the Creator. If you knew that you are experiencing the many facets of what it is to be a human being, you might view your life quite differently.

Not only would you be able to detach from your personal drama, but you would gain a sense of adventure regarding the twists and turns that appear as you move through your daily existence. Connecting with your soul wisdom expands exponentially your view of who you are and why you are here. It is like moving up a stairway and emerging on a balcony that overlooks a vast plain below where you see a panorama of events occurring simultaneously throughout time and space.

These events would show you the growth most suited for your own personal development. Knowing that you reside in a universe governed by the law of duality, it soon would become apparent that both positive and negative experiences are necessary in order for you to know what it means to be a child of God. Once you gain this awareness, all that occurs in your life is seen from a totally different perspective.

The personal pain and hurt diminishes, as does the exultation over positive events in life. It is like riding in a canoe down the river of life. You look from side to side and watch with interest what is occurring, but feel no personalized reaction to what you are seeing. You know at a deeper level that all is unfolding for your highest good, and everything is in divine order.

The Process of Reunion and Return

Much of this book centers on the nature, quality and expression of the soul or higher self. Humanity has reached the point in its evolutionary journey where it is reconnecting to the knowledge it once had regarding its true nature, which is the physical expression of an inner spiritual essence.

Currently, most individuals incarnating on the Earth plane see themselves primarily as beings living in a physical world enclosed in three-dimensional realities. They are unable to see into other realms or dimensions teeming with diverse life forms of specific purpose and expression. Even at the three-dimensional level, there are unseen beings everywhere that interact with human life on your planet.

These different realities cannot be seen or accessed because of the current belief systems prevalent on Earth today. During the past three hundred years of rational and scientific thought, the awareness of the myriad of creatures existing in our space has been lost or forgotten. However, the development of the rational, linear left hemisphere of the brain during this period was a necessary step on the soul's journey towards balance and wholeness.

Now the time has come to reconnect to the earlier knowledge, once widely held, that there are many different life forms and planes of existence available to beings incarnating on your planet. Humans are preparing to launch themselves, not only into extensive outer space travel, but also into a profound exploration of their inner space, which will require entering the realm of the soul.

Connecting to the spiritual higher self raises the level of consciousness so that multidimensional exploration can expand human capabilities. At the present time, people on your planet are living in a context, which restrains the innate abilities of all beings to progress into higher forms of life.

The primary reason for this restriction can be found in the widely held belief that all that is seen is all there is. If something cannot be seen, held or recognized in its physical reality, it simply does not exist. If the people of Earth continue in this vein, the evolution of the soul will not progress toward its final reunion with the Creator of All That Is.

Since moving on from the third dimension to a higher level of perception is a fundamental part of the process of reunion and return, it is now time for humanity to recognize that the physical body houses an eternal spark of the Creator comprised of love, wisdom and eternal life. The common name for this spark is the soul or higher self.

We grant that many people know about the existence of the soul, but very few operate continuously from that inner space, allowing it to be the master and director of life. Most human awareness stems from the activity of the brain, which sees the world in concrete, physical terms. Because this is so, the phrase "seeing through a glass darkly" is an apt description of the average experience of most people.

Seeing Life from a Different Perspective

The time of planetary transformation is here. For many eons, evolved beings within key cultures all over the planet have been doing what was needed to assist in the spiritual evolution of Earth. These great beings knew, through their higher sensing capabilities, how and where the Plan of the Creator was unfolding.

They also knew the part they were assigned to play in assisting humanity's ascension at a given point in the far distant future. They felt honored to have been selected to participate in this divine process. Even though humanity would not rise to a higher evolutionary plane during their lifetimes, the fact that they were contributing to an ongoing journey of transformation was all that mattered.

We ask that you reflect upon what we have just said here. Currently, endeavors on your planet, particularly in the western world, are primarily result-oriented. Every aspect of living is directed to accomplishing something that is recognized and measurable. The idea of contributing something to a much larger reality that takes centuries to come to fruition is foreign to the thinking of today.

Delayed gratification is considered undesirable and to be avoided at all costs. Instant satisfaction is expected in many societies all over the planet. This is one of the reasons for the anxiety experienced by many in today's world. Since this instant gratification is reached so rapidly, the sense of satisfaction for a task accomplished through perseverance and hard work is rarely achieved.

One of the most important elements of the information we bring from the realm of spirit is that each of you possesses an inner soul. This essence moves out into your world when the human persona understands that it is a part of a wider and more comprehensive reality and knows it is here to experience the many different dimensions of the Creator.

The soul has always known that it experiences multiple existences in a wide variety of realities on its journey back to reunion with the Creator. It also knows that each lifetime on Earth is like a verse in a song, which sounds a beautiful melody throughout the universes of the God Force. Once an individual in human form is able to access this level of consciousness, each lifetime is seen from a different perspective.

There is no need to finish or accomplish major themes within a lifetime. Instead there is the awareness that everything is a segment of a much greater reality, moving inexorably towards a final and far-distant conclusion. Each aspect of life is seen as contributing to something larger, and not just as an end in itself. Knowing this truth brings a deep peace and trust within the individual, which in turn impulses ever-widening circles of hope and love.

The Soul's Journey

A hunger is growing among the children of Earth regarding the possibility they might possess an immortal soul that guides and stores in memory the experiences of various lifetimes. Every human's imprint, when activated, will bring into conscious awareness who they truly are and from whence they have come. The activation comes from the center of the universe, awakening a certain number of incarnating souls in incremental cycles of time.

This activation is staged in cycles and does not occur for everyone at the same time. The Creator of All That Is intends for souls to cycle through various existences in a sequential pattern where some move forward and others remain stationary, waiting to ascend the spiral of life. Each soul starts out its journey with a deep sense of separation and alienation from Source that is almost unbearably painful.

Gradually, over eons, the individual soul becomes more and more self-sufficient—so much so that the memory of its origin fades from awareness, sinking deeply within the subconscious, waiting to be reclaimed at the appropriate time. The intent of the God Force is to send its essence into many diverse realms to reflect the wonder of what has been created.

At periodic intervals, the soul advances up the spiral of life so that a new adventure can begin. Ever so slowly, the sense of separation begins to diminish. The soul starts to feel the power of the unifying force of the Creator. The Law of Attraction pulls the soul into an interest and concern for others. The desire to be separate and alone falls away.

As the loving vibration of the Creator gains ascendancy, a desire to serve others grows within the consciousness of the soul. For the soul to have a context within which it can serve, it is necessary to have people who require assistance. The journey of souls varies from individual to individual in order to provide a framework of graduated progress for spiritual growth and development.

This current cycle will end when all the sparks of the Creator return and merge with their Source, reuniting with the Divine Essence from which they came. Then there will be a profoundly quiet period of non-existence until the next cycle of manifestation is brought into being. When we are aware of the entire process of creation from its beginning to conclusion, a deep peace permeates the core of being. We know with certainty that all truly is in divine order!

Connecting to the God Force

As we have said before, involution is the process of creation, which starts at the beginning of all life and continues on throughout vast expanses of time and space. In this way, the Divine Creator originates and continues to instill all life forms with spiritual essence. To recognize and incorporate this basic truth is to live a spiritually infused existence, continually motivated by an ongoing connection to the God Force.

Living a life connected to the Creative Power allows one to operate on an ongoing basis within an energy field that is filled with light and grace. Each and every act emanates from a calm and serene center filled with the power of the Almighty. Every act is carried out with a loving detachment that allows the individual to face what is unfolding with trust and a sense of adventure.

For life is truly a quest for adventure. When there is no ego investiture in our daily affairs, each situation can be viewed from the vantage point of an observer who delights in the great variety of interesting and absorbing experiences that occur. It is like viewing a movie as a story with no connection to the person watching, but entertaining to observe.

Most incarnating souls on the Earth plane at the present time live their lives at a deeply personal level. They think that what happens to them is part and parcel of the totality of who they are. They see themselves as separate and alone and ultimately responsible for all that is unfolding in their lives.

They do not see themselves as part of a much greater continuum that constantly expands into ever greater fields of vibratory energy, moving out into a universe full of diverse life forms. They think that they are individuals living an existence of their own making, without any other guiding principles. This view is limiting in every way.

Life in the many universes of the Creator is governed by certain immutable laws and principles, which have a direct impact on the actions of human beings—the Law of Manifestation, the Law of Cause and Effect, and the Law of Attraction, to name a few. These laws are the matrix within which everything exists. Therefore, when an individual thinks he or she alone is responsible for originating an action, there is a lack of understanding regarding the basic conditions of life.

Currently, there is little awareness of the vibratory influences constantly impacting the Earth plane. Can you see how limiting it is to exist within this framework? One of the most important tasks for us as Lightbringers is to help the inhabitants of Earth recognize that they live within a multidimensional force field flowing from the Divine Creator of All That Is.

Spiritual Practices Assisting Vibratory Transformation

Powerful vibratory energies radiate out from the center of your universe, impacting life on all dimensions. These waves of energy cannot be seen by the physical eye, for they exist at a subtle level that cannot be measured by scientific instruments. They can, however, be perceived by those who have a refined sense of intuitive knowing.

This capability is developed through a wide variety of spiritual practices that hone human sensibilities into an advanced awareness of heightened vibratory movement. Vibration and movement are the two primary qualities found on every level of existence. All molecules of life, at whatever level, exist within a matrix of vibratory waves undulating continuously throughout the universes of the Creator.

As the soul proceeds on its journey of exploration and discovery, it moves from a denser vibration to one more subtle and refined. There it is possible to gain a heightened awareness and recognition of surrounding energy fields. This progression is an essential experience on the soul's journey back to reunion with the Creator.

Many spiritual practices have originated to assist incarnating souls on the Earth plane. They have at their core the beneficial quality of raising vibrations. Some of the most effective of these practices are meditation, prayer, sacred sound and dance, contemplation, chanting, certain physical postures, attuning to nature, drumming, spinning, and immersion in water. Each of these activities raises the vibratory rates within the human body and refines its molecular structure.

For this reason, these practices have played an important role in many cultures down through time. They were recognized as having an uplifting and spiritualizing effect upon those who engaged in them. Every culture participating in any of these activities realized their value simply by the impact they had on those using them. However, very few were able to recognize the powerful changes within them that were occurring at the molecular level.

Vibratory transformation is one of the key purposes of life. As one's vibratory level rises to ever more subtle and refined states, it enhances the soul's journey back to reunion with the Creator, the primary reason for which we exist. Therefore, we ask you to incorporate these practices into your daily life. Any one of those listed above will aid you in your spiritual growth and development.

As you introduce a spiritual regimen into your life, you will notice that over time you are changing and achieving more harmony and balance in your daily affairs. A growing sense of peace begins to seep into all you do. Right action becomes easier to attain. It is as if you are a boat sailing a more steady and dependable course in life. This is possible because you have engaged in practices that have raised your vibratory state to a higher level. Is not life in its purest essence a wonder indeed?

CHAPTER 3

The Soul, A Spark of the Divine

One of the most significant advancements in evolution will be humanity's recognition and acceptance that a spiritual essence resides at the core of each body existing on the Earth plane. Life for human beings consists of a bodily form activated and upheld by a spark of spirit called the soul, which originated from within the energy field of the Creator. Physical life ceases once the soul leaves the body, ending the cycle for that incarnation.

The soul is a vibratory energy field that contains within it all the knowledge and experience gained on its long sojourn through the many dimensions of time, space and beyond. Since energy can not be destroyed, the soul does not die when the physical body expires. It leaves its current abode and proceeds to the next level, waiting to manifest whatever experience is needed for soul growth. It carries with it, however, the imprint and knowledge it has gained throughout its long journey. Its ultimate destination is reunion with the God Force that created it.

The soul is truly a child of God. It contains the fundamental nature of its creator in greatly diminished form. For this reason we have called it a spark, since it is a small essence sent out from a much greater and more powerful energy field. See in your mind's eye a gigantic fire of great heat giving off many sparks that are miniature reflections of the great being from which they have come. This analogy offers a clear picture of the relationship between the soul and the Divine Source that brought it into existence.

Why were souls created, and what is their purpose in a larger spiritual context? They originated out of the energy field of God to mirror the many facets found in all the dimensions of creation. They play the role of explorers traveling throughout the realms of spirit and matter on a sacred mission.

On this course, the soul gains knowledge and wisdom that allows it to grow into a true reflection of the Creator. The soul's divine purpose motivates it to move ever forward on its journey of exploration and discovery. The path of the soul is never static. There is always the impetus to move onward and upward towards a higher level of expression.

The underlying theme of this book is to expand humanity's awareness regarding the existence of the soul. The soul, not the intellect, is the true motivator and director of life; and the soul is connected continuously to the ultimate source of universal wisdom that created it. Thus, it is essential that all souls incarnating on the Earth plane gain the realization that they are units sent out from the God Force to grow in love and wisdom, ultimately to return to the Source from which they came.

The Soul—An Offspring of the Creator

We say it again: the soul is a unit of energy that came forth from the Mind of God. Each and every soul originated at the beginning of creation and has continued to exist down through time until the present day. We ask that you reflect upon what we have just said here, for it has great significance to you. It means that you are a physical being with an immortal soul. Your soul was activated at the outset of creation and has continued to exist through the ages, experiencing many different realms of the Creator.

You, as a soul, are an ancient being who has sought out diverse worlds to grow in the knowledge of what it means to be a child of God. The further you traveled away from the center of your origin, the more you forgot how you were formed and what your mission was. It is now time for that memory to be activated and reflect the knowledge of who you truly are.

As an offspring of the Creator, you have within your soul essence the same qualities in diminished form. You possess love, wisdom, intelligence and will—all primary attributes given to you by God. In the Divine Plan, you were meant to forget who you are and why you are here. You were to embark on a long journey to find out what it means to experience all the many elements of God's creation.

We cannot emphasize enough the importance of what we have just said here. You are on a divine journey of exploration and discovery to learn what it means to be a child of God. In order to accomplish this goal, you have had to immerse yourself in many experiences that were foreign and unknown to you in order to learn what was necessary for your soul growth.

The memory of these experiences is retained within your soul as a deep source of soul wisdom. You can call upon that wisdom at any time by simply connecting with your soul essence. By doing so, the knowledge you seek will become readily available to you. How does one connect with the wisdom of the soul?

It is so simple. Just go within to find the information gained from having lived in many different dimensions of time, space and beyond. The great teacher, Jesus, taught that the kingdom of heaven is within. He was showing the way to find one's soul. This inner pathway can be discovered simply by closing one's eyes and breathing slowly and rhythmically to quiet the mind.

Over time, an inner focus will grow that will elevate the vibratory field, allowing one to attune to and join with the soul essence. When this is accomplished, it is possible to commune directly with it and receive whatever is needed to assist with the task of daily living. The soul's primary purpose is that of love, wisdom and support for the personality, which, in turn, confronts the challenges arising in the many diverse facets of existence.

The Nature of the Soul

We would now like to delve more deeply into the nature of the soul. Once a certain portion of humanity absorbs and develops a belief in the existence of the soul, a shift of monumental proportion will occur on the Earth plane. To know that one has an essence of the Creator within one's body raises the view of life to a much higher level. This knowledge opens the gateway to multidimensional consciousness.

As long as a person thinks that life has only a physical context, it is not possible to contemplate or experience anything other than the world of matter. All life is limited to a material reality and does not include a spiritual dimension. Only that which can be seen, heard, touched or comprehended on a concrete level is considered real.

There is an ancient adage that has been repeated down through the ages, "As above, so below." Whatever we see and experience on the third dimension exists also on other unseen levels of manifestation. Just think about the implications of this saying. It is telling us that everything we encounter in our lives can be found in a similar form on other dimensional planes.

Let us look specifically at the significance of this spiritual truth. Planet Earth is peopled by a wide variety of individuals of different races, colors and cultural backgrounds. So, too, is the universe awash with differing life forms, including many who bear a resemblance to those living on your planet. Just as Earth provides different physical environments for the many diverse people on her surface, all dimensions have a context suitable for the soul experiences of those residing in them.

The soul's main purpose is to play and grow in the knowledge of what it means to be a child of God. The soul accomplishes this goal by encountering and mastering the beauty and diversity of God's creation in all its multiplicity of forms. Your current existence on Earth is being mirrored on other realms where situations like your own are unfolding, but in a different manner due to the variation in the vibratory rate.

And so it follows that souls on many different dimensions are coping with the very things you deal with in your everyday lives—how to rise up the spiral of life while encountering challenges and roadblocks that hinder and impede spiritual growth. Though these experiences differ from what is found on Earth, the impact is the same.

Since duality is a basic law of the universe, an attempt to find unity through the struggle of opposites is always occurring in some context throughout your world. The oneness of love and unity, the primary goal of the universe, can be achieved only through the embracing of that which is opposite. When one is able to become the embodiment of divine love, the power of duality will wane and disappear. Then all life will pause for a time until the next cycle of creation begins, manifesting a new theme in the divine Plan of the Creator.

Living Within a Spiritual Context

For some time now, many of Earth's inhabitants have lost a belief in the existence of an immortal soul. The primary focus has been on the mundane aspects of life with its many ups and downs. For centuries, spiritual awareness has assumed a lesser importance in the lives of most people.

This limited view is starting to change and is phasing out because of the catastrophic events occurring all over the globe. Natural disasters, war, conflict, and disruption in societal and governmental structures are bringing about a shift in the evolution of humanity on your planet. Many people are realizing at a deep level of being that their world is in the throes of dynamic disintegration.

The rapid and extensive change in the last fifty years of the twentieth century has created a lack of stability in almost every area of life, with an accompanying loss of trust in the unfolding of life as it has always been. This is particularly hard on those over fifty years of age, because they grew up in a world far different from the one that is now emerging.

Many people are feeling a deep psychic disorientation, as all that was familiar and dear is passing away before their very eyes. It is for this reason that the need to recognize oneself in a broader spiritual context is so important at this time. Therefore, a wide variety of teachers are appearing to help lead those who are lost and suffering to a belief system that will sustain them in the years ahead.

The Plan of the Creator is unfolding in its own right time. The long period of emphasis on materialism was necessary in order to anchor the soul in the human body. Now that the time for the great leap forward has arrived, spiritually infused human beings will help usher in the next evolutionary step for the inhabitants of Earth.

There is personal power in an individual who is physically grounded but also has the knowledge of his or her soul essence. Those who are aware that their immortal soul is directly connected to the Primal Source have reached a state of enlightenment, which will open the door to a higher level of consciousness.

All was in divine order during the long period of emphasis on the physical aspect of life. This age of dense materialism has served as the springboard for a new species of human being who holds the promise for a more advanced way of life. Those to come will build on the progress made by many who came before them and suffered through difficult times in order to lay the foundation for a new and better world.

The journey of the soul is like a beautiful mosaic that presents a rich and comprehensive picture of what it is to travel through the realms of the God Force. If one possessed the gift of spiritual sight, it would be possible to see the many golden skeins coming from the essence of each soul, weaving a web of vibratory energy that extends out to the farthest reaches of space.

At this time, however, most incarnating souls on the Earth plane are not able to see the connection they have with all forms of life. For eons, this ability has been submerged within the deepest recesses of the soul. When it is known that all creation is united in a vast web emanating from the Central Source of Life, an influx of the highest and most refined light will enter every area where this awareness exists.

All creation emerged from the dark energy field at the center of the universe. The recent scientific inquiry into the nature of black holes will eventually provide a greater understanding regarding the nature of God. The power existing at the center of black holes has a faint resemblance to the ultimate energy field that created all life in the many universes of time and space.

One of the most important developments of this millennium will be the growing awareness of the role that vibratory energy fields play in every aspect of life. Progress made in the field of science will prove in a concrete way what spiritual teachings have presented for centuries. As people begin to understand that all life consists of variations in the velocity and makeup of vibratory waves and particles, they will learn to direct that energy in a multiplicity of ways.

Just think of what we have said here. Once the mind is able to grasp the magnitude of its capability, human evolution will take a giant step forward. All that exists in any dimension emanates from directed mind force. When mind coalesces into single pointed intent and projects that intent outward, creation follows. Once that concept is assimilated and put into use, incarnating souls on the Earth plane will become co-creators with more highly evolved beings throughout the universe.

This greater human capability eventually will manifest in everyday life. People will expand brain capacity by moving into multidimensional consciousness. At the present time, only approximately fifteen per cent of the brain is continuously activated and operational. The human brain has the capacity to be much more sophisticated and powerful, with the ability to physically create through the power of intent alone.

The Soul's Approach to Decision-Making

When key decision-making is required in any area of life, a person aware of the existence of his or her soul begins the process in a very different way from that which is usually pursued. Before any thought or action is taken, a time for quiet introspection is set aside so that the individual can go within to connect with the soul wisdom that resides in every living being. Accessing that wisdom and bringing it into conscious awareness is the first step to be taken in any important decision-making process.

As one's consciousness moves into soul awareness, a deeper realization is reached. There is an intuitive knowing of what is for the individual's highest good at that time. This realization is the abiding theme of this process and forms the foundation for all consideration and decision-making that will follow.

Rarely do the people of Earth ask what is for their highest good as they make important choices in life. The concept is only faintly recognized at the present time. And yet the highest good is always the underlying principle for those on the journey back to the Creator. If the highest good is recognized and honored, right action will follow in all areas and will occur with ease and minimum effort.

Instead, people usually are influenced by their own emotional desires or what others feel is best for them. Even an intellectual appraisal is often missing regarding key and pivotal decisions in life. The result, therefore, is often a poor choice, followed by a fruitless effort that does not bring about the desired results. In many instances, the lack of success reflects a long-standing pattern that needs to be transmuted and released.

We wish to show you how accessing one's intuitive soul knowing needs to become part of the human decision-making process now. As one comes to acknowledge the soul residing within, everything opens up and takes on a more profound meaning. The realization dawns that we are interconnected to all life and the Source from which we came. Entering one's inner space brings a deep and abiding state of peace and security beyond what could be imagined.

So let us look at a common experience that often arises for incarnating souls on Earth's plane. It involves the question of what employment is best for one to select. At various times during life, it is necessary to make a commitment to a certain type of work in order to support physical existence. Often there are others who are dependent upon the income generated from the work chosen.

The common approach is to decide what employment the individual has training for or has an interest in. In some cases, these facts have no bearing on the decision, and the individual just looks for anything available in a given geographic area. Determining what one will do to support one's material existence is a decision of major importance. Generally, three areas of exploration are followed.

First, geographic considerations are reviewed. Does the individual want to remain in the current physical location, or will it be necessary to move somewhere else to find the right employment? Then the most suitable type of work is determined by considering education, training and experience. A mental review of these areas is thought to be essential. However, seeking a job's emotional component often plays a greater role in this process than generally recognized.

Desire, one of the strongest emotions, provides powerful motivation in any type of decision-making. What a person wants or desires often is the prime determinant for the employment pursued. In many instances, it has a stronger effect than education, training or experience. After deciding on the physical area, the line of work and the interest which brings commitment, the individual becomes more focused in identifying a specific job to solicit.

The physical activities of contact, interview and decision-making comprise the next step. If all goes well, the person is accepted, and the period of employment begins. Now most people would say that this is an accurate description of what usually occurs. The elements of physical, emotional and mental considerations are those needed to find meaningful work.

We would agree with this statement from the standpoint of three-dimensional realities. However, for those who operate from their inner soul wisdom, a very different process unfolds. This is not to say that identifying the geographic locale, the skills and abilities and the kind of work preferred would not be part of the process. All of these areas still would be fully considered.

However, an important step is missing in the example above. When one truly believes that he or she has an inner soul possessing the wisdom of the Creative Force of the Universe, the many decisions of life are determined in a very different way. One learns that vital information for successful decision-making exists within and that the highest good readily will become evident by accessing the wisdom of the soul.

Accessing Soul Wisdom

We would like to discuss a topic that is rarely broached in your world. One of the primary purposes of the soul is to address and cure not only pain and suffering it is experiencing on the Earth plane, but also healing the pain and suffering of many other souls who have dealt with the same issues.

Since all life exists within a unified field, every aspect of God's creation is interconnected within a spiritual matrix. The soul has knowledge of this connection, but human awareness of this phenomenon is lacking. One of the profound games played within the human condition is that of "hide and seek" between the soul and the human persona. Once one fuses human consciousness with the higher vibration of the soul, a greatly expanded sense of connectedness occurs.

When this ongoing soul dynamic is operating fully, the world is seen through a very different lens. There is a powerful awareness regarding the impact of every thought, word and action. We ask that you reflect on this idea for a minute. If you believed that everything you thought and did had a direct effect on a vast number of souls, would you think and act differently?

In many cases, some souls have made the commitment to enter a life in which they experience a certain level of pain and suffering in different situations. They have agreed to undergo severe trials of the kind others have had and failed to overcome. These souls are meant to withstand and to conquer these circumstances by mastering and rising above them.

Once this is accomplished, the person who has succeeded emits a powerful soul vibration of light and love that radiates out in ever-widening circles, extending into the farthest reaches of space and beyond. In this way, the soul has brought healing to all those who could not do so themselves. When one overcomes a negative pattern, energy moves out into the greater field, touching and uplifting all those who suffered from the same condition.

One of the most significant developments in the coming centuries will be the growth in awareness that each member of humanity has an indwelling soul, which is a spark of the Almighty Creator. Accessing that soul wisdom will be a valuable human capability. The practices of prayer, meditation and going within will become widespread, as the people of Earth regain what has always been their birthright.

It is for this reason that we encourage and support those of you who are in the throes of any kind of trauma. You agreed to take on this challenge for your own soul growth and knowledge; but you also committed yourself to the healing and uplifting of many other souls who are struggling or have contended with this issue in the past. Once you see that life exists within a unified field, you can move with harmony and grace to assume your rightful position as a child of God striving to serve the highest good.

When one recognizes the existence of his or her soul essence, a pivotal point in the evolutionary process has been reached. To know that one has a soul that reflects the qualities of the Divine Creator greatly expands awareness. Let us take a moment and look at how this knowledge would work in one's daily affairs.

Say that a person is suffering from a debilitating disease. There are many different healing modalities that can be pursued. The person feels adrift and unable to make a decision about which one to choose. Fear, uncertainty and panic have set in, making it very difficult to establish a positive way to proceed.

The individual goes from one possibility to another, only to end up in confusion regarding the proper decision. This happens particularly when the person has considered a variety of sources in an attempt to determine what method of healing would be best. We do not want to imply that researching and consulting others for assistance in decision-making is not valuable, because it is. However, the most successful way to make a choice in any situation is to go within and access the wisdom of the soul.

How does the process of retrieving information from the soul unfold? After the person has reviewed different types of healing and has talked with various health professionals to learn about what is available, the next step is to close the mental process of inquiry and sink into the wisdom of the soul. How does one do this? It is so simple.

Just close the eyes and breathe for a time deeply and rhythmically. Quiet the mind and attune to the peaceful emanations beginning to flow into the consciousness. If the person who is ill is willing to connect with his or her inner self and trust whatever comes forth, the next step is to ask for what is the highest good in this matter.

An intuitive knowing will come into conscious awareness. By trusting this information, a conviction grows as to what mode of healing would be the best at that time. The way forward is clear, and the individual then can embark upon the course of treatment that would be the most beneficial.

If the individual is willing to look more deeply, the cause of the illness can also be ascertained, because all physical illness stems from an imbalance residing at the emotional, psychological and, ultimately, the spiritual level. The greatest impediment to using the wisdom of the soul is a lack of trust in its accuracy. This trust can be achieved by having constant contact with the soul through quiet attunement and then by observing and testing the reliability of the wisdom received.

After gaining insight from the soul, every aspect of the being takes on a higher mode of expression. Trusting in the rightness of one's actions, no matter what the outcome, brings a peace and harmony to life beyond what can be imagined. One's view of life expands and assumes a spiritual dimension, raising one up to a higher level of expression.

The Soul and the Dying Process

We would like to speak with you now about what the soul experiences during and after the dying process. When the time of death arrives, no matter what the form of leaving, a fundamental inner shift occurs before the actual departure. The soul's knowing that death is imminent is released into the human body, particularly through the right hemisphere of the brain and a space within the heart.

This awareness can come in the minutes before death or much earlier, depending on the manner in which death occurs. The individual's level of consciousness plays a significant role in how this process unfolds. When one dies quickly or violently, the knowledge that it is time to depart the Earth plane comes during and immediately following release from the body.

In the case of a lingering illness, a different process occurs. The individual has time to review the life and gain realization regarding its purpose and the degree to which that purpose was achieved. When death comes slowly, there is the opportunity to connect with the realm of spirit and reflect back to those living on Earth the many higher-dimensional realities the dying person is seeing.

Loved ones who are watching someone near and dear to them die in what appears to be lingering and painful ways do not comprehend how uplifting this process really is. They are generally unaware that the soul is being refined through the density of third-dimensional suffering, resulting in the ascension to a higher spiritual level.

Pain that is physical, emotional or psychological provides the needed catalyst for spiritual growth. This is why all souls reside for some time on the third dimension, so they can accelerate their soul growth through the powerful vibrational field that exists there. For those of our readers who are suffering during an extended dying process or are participating in this experience with someone else, we ask that you expand your perspective on what is happening.

Look at death as the completion of but one chapter in a long and beautiful account of the soul's journey. Know that life is the process by which the soul experiences many diverse aspects of the human condition. Understand that there is no beginning and no end to the life of the soul. Everything in the universe is energy in motion. Learn from this experience. Grow in your knowledge of what it is to be a child of God on a journey of ultimate reunion with your Creator.

To become a truly realized being, the soul must walk the various pathways of life. The soul gathers wisdom and knowledge through many lifetimes experiencing the different elements of what it is to be human. One of the most significant lessons to be learned is how to deal with pain, which the third dimension features very powerfully. When pain is viewed from the soul's perspective, a spiritual step of great magnitude has been taken.

One of the most significant events the soul experiences during any incarnation is that of dying. Through many lifetimes, death comes in a variety of ways. The soul will have lives that are brief or lives of different lengths, but each will contain a lesson learned regarding the human condition.

For the soul who lives a short time, the value of life will be the paramount truth to be gleaned from such a brief existence. The knowledge regarding the value of life will be carried by the soul at a deep intuitive level into all other incarnations. When one lives into full maturity and old age, one has the time to gain understanding, which develops into abiding wisdom.

Those who die peacefully and with full consciousness will emerge after passing over with complete comprehension of the spiritual context within which they lived. This awareness will settle into the broader soul-knowing of what it means to travel throughout the many dimensions of the Creator. This knowledge will then be carried forward into future lifetimes.

When one dies a quick and violent death, the soul experiences a period of deep sleep, all the while being lovingly attended to by those whose role it is to assist the traumatized in passing over to the realm of spirit. Every individual soul is a spark of the Source from which it came and is precious, no matter how it has lived.

Each universe is a self-contained interactive unit teeming with a myriad of life forms, all valued and cared for by spiritual forces assigned by the Creator. The human emotions of loneliness and separation are an illusion that does not reflect the true reality of life. If an individual could sense the spiritual beings that are always in proximity, it would be impossible to feel the isolation so common in today's world.

It is for this reason that this book concentrates on the nature and experiences of the soul. Those living on Earth need to know that they possess a unit of divine energy that never dies—one that is connected to all life within the universe and ultimately to the God Force. Once this conviction is reached, life expands, illuminating every element of existence.

The term "self-realization" has been used in religious and spiritual teachings to define a state of elevated consciousness. The reality of this state can be found in what we have been discussing here. When one becomes aware of the existence of his or her soul and that it is moving through a myriad of experiences in God's creation, a form of self-realization has been reached. From this expanded state, co-creation with the God Force can begin.

Ascending to a Higher Vibratory State

You now can see more clearly the thread of ideas we are bringing forth for your consideration. We are presenting a more expansive look at what it means to be a soul encased in physical form evolving through a series of life experiences on Earth's plane. Our primary emphasis is to increase awareness of your spiritual origin and what the journey back to that origin entails.

In earliest times on your planet, inhabitants of Earth knew that they were spiritual beings playing in the fields of matter to reflect back to Source what it means to be human. They felt at the deepest levels of their being this connection and constantly attuned through rituals and practices to their Divine Source.

Because they knew who they were and from whence they had come, they had a greater brain capacity, enabling them to function with a speed and comprehension far beyond that of human beings in your present day. Tuning in to a greatly magnified power source requires physical strength and a multiplicity of pathways in the brain just to contain the power of the energy field. It is essential that one not be harmed by the intense emissions from a higher realm.

Human beings, in present times, are just beginning to reawaken to the enormity of what it means to be a conductor of spiritual energies, which vibrate at a higher rate in certain individuals. They are becoming aware of the necessity for toning and strengthening their physical bodies, as well as expanding their mental abilities so that they can contain the powerful stream of energy engulfing them.

Many people are placing an important emphasis upon refining their physical bodies. They need to develop tensile strength, which allows them to bend but not break as vibratory waves from the center of the galaxy increase ten-fold in the coming years. For this reason, many individuals currently are dealing with severe health problems that appear suddenly and with very little warning. We would like to reassure our readers that all is in divine order, no matter what the outcome of these illnesses might be.

The planet and those who live on her surface are going through a massive release, which will refine and renew all life preparing for the next evolutionary step on Earth. The time for this great shift in human consciousness is here, and certain basic changes must be made to assure the success of this shift. The primary one must be the release of all darkness, density and negativity, wherever it exists.

Illness is reflected as a dark area in the body's energy field, which must be cleared and restored to positive functioning in order for true health to exist. In certain locales on Earth, powerful negative vortexes exist. This is due to the planet's energy field, the result of actions by those residing in that area, or both. It is for these reasons that warfare seems to appear in certain areas of the globe and not in others.

Many of you have descended into the deepest part of your being to bring into conscious awareness the great pain you have been carrying with you for a number of lifetimes. In this lifetime, you agreed at a soul level before entering the Earth plane that you would take upon yourself the rigorous process of release and healing, so that you could ascend to a higher vibratory state.

Many incarnating souls currently living on the Earth plane are going through this process, for this is the end of an expanse of time on your planet. Many are beginning to realize what it means to be an essence of the Creator, living within a physical body while moving towards reunion with its Divine Source.

In order for this merging with Source to occur, it has been necessary for individual sparks of spirit to travel far and wide through the many dimensions of time and space within the universes of the Almighty. The entire purpose of this long and arduous journey has been to experience God's creation in its many different forms.

In this divine game of hide and seek, the soul immerses itself in a certain continuum, and then emerges to find its true essence and nature. The soul is a part of the Universal Consciousness many call God. A number of holy scriptures have reflected this truth by saying that humankind was created in the image of God, a profound truth existing at the core of creation.

Another prime reality regarding the soul, little known and rarely recognized, is that the soul is always connected to the Creative Source, which constantly replenishes and supports its beloved offspring. There are spiritual traditions that describe this phenomenon as a golden stream of light—one that can never be broken. There are periods when the individual soul is conscious of this contact with its Creator and other times when it is not.

The inhabitants of Earth are emerging from eons when this knowledge has been lost. One of the major developments of this millennium will be the retrieval of the ancient wisdom regarding the eternal spark of spirit within every human being that is directly linked to the Source from which it came. We ask that you reflect upon the magnitude of what we have just said.

To see oneself within this greater context will cause incarnating souls to ascend up the spiral of life and move ever closer to that eventual time of reunion with the God Force. A human being operating out of an awareness of his or her spiritual essence will move into a greatly expanded capacity for life. All the lower emotions of fear, grief, anger and guilt cannot exist in this rarified vibratory field. The natural state of elevated consciousness, which is love and joy, is the true nature of the Creator and the birthright of every incarnating soul.

CHAPTER 4

Birthing a New World

Your world has begun its journey into dark and chaotic times. There have been many periods on your planet when those living within the third dimension have entered an intense evolutionary phase where they experienced increased pain and suffering. The people of Earth are now entering another one of these periods.

We ask that you take some deep and rhythmic breaths. See yourselves encased in a beautiful golden light, which warms and relaxes you at all levels. Go within to your soul essence and bask in its love and wisdom. For your soul is all-knowing and can see the positive aspects of what we say with the breadth and comprehension of spirit.

The Great Purification

A time of profound global change has begun for the inhabitants of your planet. One of the major developments for this century and beyond will be the shift to a new area of geographic dominance. All life on Earth moves in a westward motion. This phenomenon allows different people in a variety of locales to experience a new cycle of human growth and spiritual development.

If you review the history of the cultures on your planet, this westward movement is readily evident. Recently, the United States has been the preeminent power on Earth, having held this role for some time. America's position as the strongest national power in the world has reached its peak and is starting to wane.

The United States is moving into the descending phase of its political cycle. The importance it holds will diminish ever so slowly until its time of completion is achieved. This country has accomplished the task of introducing democracy to the world at large. The United States is the first political entity to provide a model for this form of government on such a wide scale.

Once the purpose for a people is accomplished, a decline begins that prevents a return to the heights already achieved. This is a recurring pattern that has been in existence since the earliest days of intelligent life on your planet. Cyclical movement can be found in all life forms in the many universes of time, space and beyond. Once something begins, it eventually returns to the point where it started in order to achieve completion.

Many indigenous cultures have woven this concept into their ceremonies and rituals. Native Americans used the medicine wheel to place themselves symbolically during the various phases of their lives. The medicine wheel represented the personal cycle in visual form, which showed them where they were as they moved forward on their life's path.

Lack of knowledge concerning the significance of cycles causes people to lose sight of their rhythms and patterns. They are cut adrift from their rightful place in the overall scheme of things. Knowing where one is and where one is headed on a larger scale provide security and peace on an inner level, which is important for the incarnating soul. A deeper understanding and acceptance become the guiding force in life.

With this awareness in mind, we would like to return to the westward movement of ascendancy on your planet. The next area on Earth rising again to political and cultural dominance will be the Pacific Rim countries, China and India. New life expressions will surface in these countries providing advanced spiritual growth, which will infuse energy into that which has been accomplished in the past.

We do not wish to imply that these areas of Earth will not be touched by the physical changes occurring elsewhere. Those residing in these lands will have to face the challenges of a planet in the throes of shifting and altering land masses, just as others will be doing all over the globe. In time, however, the Earth changes will lessen, and a more normal period of development will begin.

For eons, the wise elders of Earth foretold a great process of purification that would come at the end of an age when humanity had sunk into dense materialism. They knew that the cleansing and healing would demand much of the people and strain them to their limits. For this reason, there have been those throughout Earth's history who have assisted in preparing for this process.

The indigenous peoples on your planet have always known what was coming and have kept the information alive through an oral tradition, which was very specific about what would occur. These people live primitively but, nevertheless, have a profoundly complex and sophisticated awareness about their planet, the galaxy and the universe. They have fulfilled the role of Guardians of the Flame by keeping this sacred knowledge alive down through the centuries.

In recent decades, these indigenous people have released this long-held information in order for the general public to know what was about to occur. We, a group soul, are also bearers of this information, so that the people of Earth can understand what they are experiencing and why.

Indigenous people have always viewed their existence as an integral part of a sacred circle. They understood the concept of cyclical life, which provided them with a sense of security and peace as they faced difficult times. They knew that after the storm the rainbow of renewed life would unfold on a higher level of the spiral, giving them the courage to face the hardships they were about to endure.

All inhabitants of Earth have, at some time, lived in an indigenous culture where this view of life was imprinted on the matrix of the soul. Every one of you carries knowledge regarding the cyclical aspect of existence. We ask you to call upon that awareness, as we look at the process of purification, which is beginning in earnest all over your globe. It is particularly important at this time to see events from an expanded spiritual viewpoint, to help one comprehend what is about to occur.

Indigenous people all over the planet have kept alive a long-held tradition regarding this period in humanity's evolution. The Great Purification has been spoken and sung about for eons. It was prophesied and held within the sacred teachings of many who knew that it was their duty to carry forth this knowledge, so that those who would come after them would be informed of the intense global changes to engulf the planet at a distant time in the future.

The elders and teachers found within all cultures in the past had access to the wisdom of the higher dimensions through sophisticated means of meditation and attunement. They possessed the ability to view vast stretches of time, which they then incorporated into the oral and written traditions of their people.

Because of this ability, they knew that the inhabitants of Earth would descend into an extended period of dense materialism typified by greed, corruption and warfare, identified in the Hindu tradition as the Kali Yuga. The Native American people have long talked of a time of great suffering, which would then be followed by purification in all areas of life.

As we have said before, many cycles on Earth are coming to a close, the most extensive of which is one of 500,000 years. Humanity is ready to move forward to a more advanced form of functioning. Therefore, it is necessary to wash away the debris and undesirable elements of the past so that a new world can emerge and provide a compatible environment for the species of human being waiting to enter Earth's plane.

The Native American elders know that we have moved into the period of the Great Purification, so long relayed by those exalted ones who came before them. They tell us that it will be necessary to clean the slate in preparation for the emergence of a New World. Since many of their own people have fallen away from the core of their prophetic teachings, it is a lonely road for those who stay true to the ancient wisdom.

The knowledge about the Great Purification, however, has been released into the awareness of many throughout the planet. We also offer this information as a guide for the times ahead. To possess a firm conviction that life on this planet is ever evolving to a higher state of consciousness will help you accept and understand the underlying good that is unfolding within the dissolution and destruction in every corner of your world.

We wish to describe in concrete, practical terms what this process will entail for those living on your planet. Purification or cleansing will occur in many different areas of life and will manifest ultimately as healing—a process long overdue and sorely needed. To see the purification process as positive will be of great assistance in the times ahead.

First, we will speak about planetary purification, which is emerging within ever accelerating events all over Earth. Long periods of habitation by many different cultures have left a vibratory residue of negativity that must be removed in order for new, more advanced people to come forth and raise humanity to a higher level of functioning. Also, the land masses require reconfiguration so that a fresh, unsullied physical environment can support the civilizations that are to come.

The soul entity inhabiting your planet recognizes this need and has been raising her vibratory field as well. In order for momentous change to be accomplished, she will continue to experience severe natural disasters and general climatic upheavals. They will serve as a vehicle for spiritual transformation for her, as well as for those living on her surface.

For some time into the future, all areas of Earth will experience flooding, earthquakes, volcanic eruptions or severe disturbances in local weather patterns. We ask that those of you living during these turbulent times adopt as positive a view as possible by comparing these events to the birthing process. The natural disasters occurring all over Earth are similar to the labor pains experienced when a newborn child is brought into the world.

The pain and suffering accompanying the birth process are considered well worth it once the newborn child arrives. So it is with the birthing of the New World. In future years, there will be difficult events that will try the souls of those living on your planet. It simply cannot be avoided. Physical purification will be carried out through the elements of fire and water—two of the four primary forces in your universe.

Planetary transformation is causing the overheating of Earth, which is melting the polar ice caps. In this century and the one following, many occupied areas along sea coasts will be inundated and submerged. The loss of land masses to higher water levels has happened many times in the past, engulfing centers of civilization that were more advanced than those currently existing on Earth.

We ask that you face these Earth changes with a sense of equanimity and inner poise. The deep distress caused by tumultuous climatic change is necessary in order to purify the planet and welcome the new human species waiting to be born. Hold this thought ever with you as you move through the disruption and dislocation of the years ahead.

Raising Earth's Vibration

Much is unfolding on Earth as the vibratory field of your planet increases in intensity and volume. Many different factors are contributing to this situation. First and foremost, the spiritual entity inhabiting your planet is raising her vibration to accompany the evolutionary step humanity is taking on its journey back to Source.

In order to raise her vibratory field, she is calling upon fire to assist her in this herculean task. In all cultures, fire has been associated with spiritual beings and ultimately the Divine Creator. As the element of fire is gaining force, Earth is entering into the crucible of death and transformation that accompanies it. This is reflected in the increase in temperature, volcanic activity, and earthquakes occurring all over the planet.

There are other reasons, of course, for the changes we have just described. Earth's tectonic plates are constantly shifting and adjusting during recurring cycles of cooling and warming through the millennia. Also, the unbridled use of technology, with no commitment to using only what enhances the wellbeing of the planet, has increased the heat emitted by your planet.

We ask that you consider what we have said here. Beyond the physical reasons for climate change, there is a higher spiritual purpose unfolding. Gaia, the name we choose to use for this great being that infuses your planet with her essence, is willingly experiencing great pain and upheaval deep within herself to assist humanity on its spiritual journey.

She knows the land upon which you walk must be irradiated to hold a higher vibration in order to be in harmony with the new, advanced species coming onto the Earth plane in greater and greater numbers. The heat generated from her travail is contributing to momentous planetary changes. Volcanoes and earthquakes restructure land masses so that fresh soil can incubate and enrich those who will occupy them.

There is a growing sense of despair among the inhabitants of Earth as they witness the devastating impact of climate and temperature change. Many feel helpless and are beginning to wonder if they are witnessing the death throes of the planet. Nothing could be farther from the truth. It is important to recognize and honor the process Gaia is going through. Know that it is happening for a higher purpose—that of transformation and rebirth so that another more advanced cycle of human evolution can occur.

Do whatever you can to mitigate the agony Gaia has taken on for your benefit. Join in the growing awareness for the need to connect to Mother Earth. Develop an environmental consciousness and commitment and support only those actions that contribute to the wellbeing of your planet. Refuse to accept the decisions of government or industry when they run counter to what is the highest good for Gaia. She is the ultimate mother of us all and deserves no less than our complete love and respect.

Interconnectedness of Life

We now ask that you consider the reality that all forms of life on Earth are interconnected. One concrete example of this is our advanced communications technology, which makes it possible for anyone to view catastrophic weather conditions firsthand as they unfold in different locales on the planet.

Witnessing a severe weather condition while it is occurring affects one at a deeply subconscious level. This is because memories of similar events from other lifetimes are stored within the subconscious. These memories may be triggered and released while watching something similar on a television screen.

You may ask how this could be. To prove the validity of our statement, we ask the reader to become quiet and go within for a brief moment. Ask your subconscious mind to release into your awareness the memory of any violent weather condition you experienced in another time or place.

For many, you may see a coastline ringed with flames. Others may see inundations of water, the collapsing of mountains because of an earthquake, or the deadly explosion of a volcano destroying all life in a given area. A scene of something other than what we have suggested here may come into your mind. Just accept what surfaces with detached equanimity.

If you are able to connect with your subconscious mind, you may bring up a picture or knowing about a life experience where you were involved in a catastrophic disaster. The incarnating soul carries memories of traumatic events from lifetime to lifetime because of the lasting emotional impact of what has occurred.

It is for this reason that many currently living on Earth carry a deep-seated sense of anxiety, or even dread, and are unaware of its existence. It resides at a low level of inner knowing that may surface when any similar catastrophe is witnessed or read about. To determine whether this condition exists deep within your psyche, stop and quietly go within the next time you see or hear about any type of natural disaster.

Ask your subconscious mind to release the knowledge of what you have experienced into your conscious awareness, so that you can eliminate the emotional charge you are carrying. What we are asking you to do here is extremely important. A traumatic experience with its corresponding emotional charge, carried deep within the subconscious, can be extremely debilitating.

Many inhabitants of Earth are being caught in severe natural disasters. When this happens and one had previously experienced a similar traumatic event, the shock can affect the individual so profoundly that the ability to respond to the crisis is severely diminished. Many shut down and descend into a semi-catatonic state, unable to rise to what is needed at the time.

We bring this matter to your attention so that you can release the emotional shock and trauma being held within your subconscious mind and be ready to face severe weather conditions if and when they impact you. This is an issue of major importance, because almost every corner of your planet will be going through various stages of upheaval during turbulent climatic conditions in the coming decades.

We ask that you look at your life through a wider lens. All is unfolding on your planet in harmony with the divine Plan of the Creator. Everything that exists in the many universes of time and space does so within a prescribed matrix, which is brought into being first on the level of Idea. Idea carries with it the highest vibration found in all creation. It comes directly from the Mind of God and carries with it the intent of the Primal Force of the Universe.

Why do we speak about an abstract, metaphysical concept that may be beyond the comprehension of most humans on the Earth plane at the present time? We do so to infuse you with the awareness that this information is within your ability to absorb and understand. People living in the three-dimensional realm of your planet are in the process of taking a great step forward in the evolutionary journey toward Source.

For many centuries of time on Earth, the realization of the ongoing connection between the realms of spirit and the plane of matter has lain dormant in the subconscious memory banks of most inhabitants. In the earliest days of human life on your planet, incarnating souls were aware of the connection between themselves and the higher realms, and they accessed them on an ongoing basis. As the density of the Earth plane increased, the knowledge weakened and finally was lost.

Now in this twenty-first century, that profound awareness is returning slowly but inexorably to those living throughout your planet. Some are beginning to see entities, as well as actual places and events that are occurring in other realms of existence. Many here on Earth are developing a sixth sense and sight regarding their world, which is rich with an extensive variety of life forms.

As these abilities increase, the inhabitants of Earth will expand in brain capacity, physical health, strength and extrasensory perception regarding the world around them. Whatever they concentrate on will grow and progress more quickly and extensively than it does at the present time. As quantum physics teaches, the focusing of attention is the initial act of creation. When the power of intent is added, it provides the catalyst for a higher level of manifestation.

One of the primary laws of the universe is the Law of Manifestation. We described it in *The Higher Dimensions—Our Next Home* and would like to repeat what we said there. This law is a basic principle operating in the world of matter and provides the framework within which physical creation occurs. Anything brought into being at the third-dimensional level does so within the context of the Law of Manifestation.

The process begins at the level of mental causation or idea. It then moves to the emotional level of desire, which combines energy and commitment, and finally enters the realm of physical reality where the actual expression occurs. In the future, humans will be able to manifest by just envisioning what they want to create. It then will come into being through the power of their mind force.

A Time of Great Change

Life as those of you on Earth know it is approaching an end. Great changes are in the offing, changes that will bring about a transformation in the way you live. Societal and governmental structures will experience major transformations, realigning existence in many different ways. Many cultures will be modified greatly or disappear altogether.

At the present time, government plays a controlling role in most countries. A very few individuals dominate and dictate the major areas of life, with little consideration for the wishes of the vast majority of people. In fact, the popular will is generally manipulated or ignored by those in positions of power. This condition has been the norm for many eons on your planet.

As the feminine principle continues to ascend, governmental dominance will shift to a more responsive stance in regard to the needs of the people. The general populace will insist that the government be accountable and meet the needs of its citizens. Political power will flow from the hands of the few to rest with the many, irrevocably changing the manner in which people are governed.

This process is already underway in countries all over the globe. Governments that are operating under dictatorial conditions are losing their influence and are starting to crumble. Misuse of power is being challenged, as people rise up and insist that governing become more egalitarian. One of the most significant movements presently occurring in your world is the rising status of women and minorities.

For many centuries now, the male principle has been in ascendance, causing women much pain and suffering. In some countries, women are still considered chattel and have no personal rights or privileges. This situation is changing at a basic molecular level. The indwelling feminine essence of your planet is raising her vibratory rate in preparation for the more highly evolved species that will be coming soon.

This species will contain the feminine and masculine principles in a state of balance and harmony within each individual. Respect and consideration will prevail in relationships between men and women. Domination and control will be considered abhorrent behavior and will not be supported in any way. Governments will reflect this new approach and will function in service to the people rather than as the master who must be obeyed at all costs.

The changes we have just described will take time to grow and develop. Generations will struggle to achieve this higher mode of functioning in all areas of life. There will be much trial and error along the way, but the important thing to know is that the energy of the old traditions is waning and will not sustain things as they have been.

More and more, attempts to dominate and control will fail. This new way can be compared to the power of a great wave that cannot be stopped or contained. Feel the force of what is manifesting and help to bring it into being. By so doing, you will be helping to create a New World.

In this century and those to come, there will be shifts and changes in the political makeup of many countries around the globe. Established governments will fall or be transformed at a fundamental level. The energy field of Earth will no longer uphold power politics or governments that operate within a dictatorial framework.

The welfare and will of the people is increasing in power and force, and citizens will replace those governments that do not respond to their needs. Many women will move into meaningful roles in business, industry and government. This trend is already underway in many western nations. A gentler, more feminine approach to life will prevail, as male and female energies achieve balance and harmony.

There will be a radical transformation in the use of military force in the years ahead. The continuous warfare of the twentieth and twenty-first centuries will abate, and it will no longer be acceptable to settle disputes between nations through acts of war. People will question, as never before, the loss of human life and the squandering of valuable resources. New systems will develop to resolve conflicts in a fair and peaceful way.

When more and more individuals on Earth adopt the spiritual practice of connecting with their soul essence, strife and war will become intolerable. The basic spiritual energy of the universe is love—the antithesis of what is found when people and nations quarrel and physically attack each other. A dense and dark vibration is emitted wherever these situations exist.

The people of the future will be more refined psychologically and emotionally and will not tolerate the lowering of their energetic field through negative interactions with others. As Earth raises her vibratory level, the energetic framework for conflict and war will dissipate and finally disappear. The people of your planet will rise up the spiral of life and will join others in the galaxy awaiting their arrival.

People on Earth are not alone. Your universe contains many different kinds of life and consciousness. Down through the ages, there have been ongoing accounts of the many visitors from outer space who have come to your planet to assist in your evolutionary development. Since they have mastered interplanetary travel and have not been restricted to the time constraints imposed by the speed of light, many beings from a wide variety of star systems have come to your planet throughout the eons.

There are depictions of them in the artwork found on rocks and in caves all over the planet. Often they have guided the human race and even intervened in upgrading its physical and mental development. The children of Earth carry deep within their genetic structure the imprint of these galactic visitors. One of the greatest advancements for humanity will occur when contact is finally made with the space brothers and sisters who have interacted with the children of Earth since earliest times.

New Locales for Spiritual Advancement

Certain areas of the planet will be gaining in influence during this century and beyond. The countries on the western end of the Pacific Rim, China, India and portions of eastern Asia are slowly moving into a preeminent position within the family of nations and will be in ascendancy for an extended time.

Innovative cultures emerging in these areas will join with those that already exist, providing fertile ground for spiritual advancement. Life experiences in these regions will add a new dimension to the human condition. New cultural values and customs will provide a rich background for those incarnating in these locales.

Life will continue throughout the planet, but the geographic areas containing the greatest vibrancy and opportunities for humanity on its evolutionary path will appear in the locations we have mentioned above. We offer this information as a glimpse into the future, so that those who are thinking of moving to new areas on Earth can reflect upon what we have said.

In the twentieth century, warfare caused multiple migrations, which generally brought people to new lands distant from their homes. In the twenty-first century, people will start to move all over the globe because of climate change, adverse weather conditions, natural disasters, and warfare. People will travel far and relocate in lands foreign to them.

Adapting to unfamiliar environments creates stress on the body, mind and spirit. Becoming accustomed to a totally new environment breaks down old patterns of behavior and causes people to explore new and different means of existence. Some people will retain their old customs, but many will help form societies based on innovative and previously untried ways of living.

We ask that you keep in mind what we have just said. The movements of people throughout Earth will be a type of human fertilization for the planet. Those forced to leave their countries, or those whose pioneering spirit is the motivating factor, are like farmers tilling the soil for a new crop. They will be cultivating and providing the humus for emerging cultures that will appear and prosper in the centuries ahead.

If people who leave their homeland can view themselves in a more expanded manner and recognize the monumental shift occurring in humanity's evolution, relocation will be much easier. They will be able to release the memories of their previous life and turn their attention to the exciting task ahead, breaking ground for a new and better world.

Children of Earth need to see themselves and their world as a part of an extended journey of reunion with the Creator. It is time to recognize that the raising of consciousness and the upward movement of the soul is an ongoing process of continual forward motion. Therefore every experience is worthwhile and contributes to the highest good.

As Gaia, the spiritual entity impulsing your planet, continues her process of transformation, alterations in the surface of Earth will grow in magnitude and violence. Storms of increasing velocity will be the catalyst bringing about these changes. Earthquakes, volcanic activity and raging fires are occurring with greater frequency.

The two primary forces of fire and water are modifying the topography of the planet and will continue to do so for centuries. The continents where human habitation has been the densest will be the most affected, because these lands need to be prepared for a new and different species of human being. The greatest changes will occur north of the equator.

This is so for a number of reasons. A majority of human advancement has occurred north of the equator on your planet. Since the cycles for the cultures in these regions are coming to an end, their negative energy must be cleansed and freed. Also, much of the warfare currently conducted on Earth has taken place in these areas. Strife and conflict must be eliminated at a vibratory level.

Therefore, North America, Europe, the Near East, Asia and some islands in the Pacific Ocean will be torn asunder in certain locales. The maps of the future will be very different than those of today. The lands next to oceans, rivers, large lakes, fault lines and some mountain ranges will be modified and changed.

The Southern Hemisphere will not go unscathed during this process. Certain portions of continents will be lost for further habitation while others will increase in size. Some will sink below the oceans' waves, as new land that has been lying fallow for centuries will rise to be used again. We will not speak of specific changes since even Mother Earth herself does not know completely how her surface will look in the future. All is a work in progress.

What we can say with certainty is that people living on the planet should develop the view that momentous change may be coming into their lives in some form or another. It will be important to have the capacity to flow with the changes that will be coming. Clinging to the security of what has existed in the past will be a dangerous position to hold, since the current way of life will be greatly altered all over the planet.

It is possible, however, to ride the wave of planetary transformation in a state of high well-being. One can do this by believing that the changes occurring are ultimately for humanity's highest good. Trust and faith in the unfolding of God's Plan will provide the support needed to deal with and accept the displacements that may follow. Again we emphasize the importance of connecting to the soul essence within. It will give you wisdom and strength to meet the challenges that will appear in your life.

As your world is about to embark upon a period of massive upheaval in all areas, the time for restructuring down to the most basic level is about to begin. For those who value security and the status quo, the period we are describing will be a most difficult one indeed. The winds of change are sweeping over Earth, destroying the old paradigm and bringing into being a new and totally different way of living.

We would like to spend some time covering the many areas that will be impacted by this great change. First, we shall dwell upon the condition of your mother planet herself. Earth is inhabited by a being of great spiritual power. It is her energy field that supports and sustains the many life forms on her surface.

She is going through a great initiation, which is altering all levels of her consciousness. This transformation is changing her electromagnetic energy field, which means that the vibrations emanating from her core will change. They will contain higher molecular frequencies that will impulse everything existing on her surface.

Ultimately the current land masses will modify to accommodate the new energy infusing them. The Northern Hemisphere of the globe will be changed the most in the coming centuries. There will be extensive flooding and reconfiguration of the land, which will result in the ocean covering many currently inhabited areas.

These changes are necessary because the energy remaining from many dark and destructive events that have occurred in the countries of the Northern Hemisphere needs to be cleansed and washed away. New lands will arise both in the north and south, offering a fresh start for those coming onto the Earth plane. There will be mass migrations of people from geographic areas unfavorably impacted by adverse weather conditions or ongoing warfare.

Also, more people will be able to tune into the energy field in which they live. If it contains the residue of negative vibrations from past events, they may chose to relocate to a more energetically favorable place. Large groups of people will be immigrating to places they never thought possible. This process will result in a cross-pollination of Earth's people, creating a new mixture of individual characteristics and races. This fusion of human traits and capabilities will produce an advanced human being who will lead the people of Earth to a higher plane of evolutionary development.

So we ask you to recognize that you are living in lands that may no longer be able to support the life you are currently living. Broaden your view of who you are and where it is best for you to reside. Try to identify the quality of the vibrational field in which you live. Do you feel a positive sense of harmony and well-being where you now reside? Access your soul knowing to find the answer to this question.

If it does not feel positive, that may be an indication that you are not being supported energetically by your current locale. If so, continuing to reside there may not be in your best interest. In the future, many of the people of Earth will determine where they will live solely on the basis of the vibrational aspects of a given geographic energy field.

We want you to be aware of the primary forces and events that will prevail in the twenty-first century and beyond. To do so, it is necessary to understand how life unfolds on your planet. The evolutionary path of humanity on Earth is constantly impulsed by vibratory waves of energies that affect those on the planet's surface in certain measurable and recognizable ways.

There is intelligence and power in these vibratory waves, which emanate from the center of the universe. Divine intent contained within these energy fields touches and impacts everything on the planet. The unseen power behind all life is the spiritual will of the God Force assisting creation throughout the many dimensions of time, space and beyond. How the intent manifests depends on the free will of the life forms affected.

Because of free will, a wide variety of different outcomes can emanate from the same pulsation of energy. The Source of All Life has given the gift of free will to intelligent creation, which guarantees diversity in how the impulse manifests. For this reason, it is very difficult to prophesy with accuracy the exact time and place certain events will occur, since people always have a choice in how to use the spiritual energy impacting them.

It is possible, however, for us to give the inhabitants of Earth a general view of the unseen forces, which will be affecting humanity during the physical transformation of the planet. At periodic intervals in the past, Earth's continents and land masses have experienced great convulsions and upheavals. There always is a divine purpose in destruction of land to complete the life cycle of a culture whose experiences have been supported by the area where they live.

As the cycle for a particular group of people draws to a close, the devastation of their physical environment clears the way for souls waiting to enter the Earth plane. The land needs to be reconfigured to suit what is to come. Since your entire planet is preparing for a more advanced form of human expression, a massive physical restructuring will be necessary to provide the environment needed for incoming souls.

These Earth changes will start to surface in the twenty-first century and will continue for centuries to follow. Water levels will rise, inundating land along the coasts of all countries. Many towns and cities will sink below the waves and will be faint memories in the future—a phenomenon that has occurred many times in the past.

The inundations will cause movements of large groups of people seeking new homes on higher ground. These migrations will result in the intermingling of people and cultures, creating new races with genetic traits and characteristics unlike those of the past. These people will inhabit lands cleansed and reconfigured by water, earthquakes or volcanic activity. They will live and imprint their own vibratory pattern on a new cycle of evolutionary growth.

Prophecy—A Story of Probable Futures

During this current period on Earth, there is a growing interest in prophecy, as people try to deal with uncertainty in all walks of life. The desire to know what the future may hold is important to many who are charting a new and different course in the face of tremendous change. We would like to shed some light on this matter of prophecy.

At the outset of creation, a blueprint for all life was established by the Primal Source. Within that blueprint, however, fluid movement provided a variety of probable futures, depending on the choices made by participating souls. One of the great gifts the God Force gave the souls it created was free will. All life is governed by two basic principles—the foundational blueprint created by God and the free will choices made by each soul.

For this reason, it is important to comprehend the underlying nature of prophecy. The future is merely a template that can be modified by those participating in it at any given time. Always keep this in mind when receiving information about "future events." Anything existing within the original blueprint can be changed by incarnating souls exercising their free will.

Prophecy can be helpful when viewed as a description of probable futures. Upon hearing about something that is yet to occur, know that it can be impacted by the focusing of free will and intent. It might be helpful to view prophecy as a spiritual weather report presenting climatic conditions that can be changed by an infusion of new energy different from that which has been anticipated.

Currently there is great interest in the prophecies of the ancient Mayans. They developed a system of observation that charted your solar system on its journey within a spiral arm of your galaxy. Earth currently is moving through a portion of your galaxy in alignment with its center. With an accuracy rarely seen until now, the Mayans were able to identify the placement of your planet over great spans of time as it moved through its galaxy.

The Mayans knew that part of their responsibility as a people was to record your planet's position in relationship to your galaxy. To them it was a sacred duty given to them by the Creator. Their elders were able to travel to higher realms to bring back to their people a description of the tasks they were being asked to perform.

Certain individuals were trained in the observation and recording of Earth's placement as it related to the movement within the larger galactic community. Currently, people on your planet view the solar system and the galaxy as separate entities, with very little understanding of their interrelationship.

The Mayans developed the ability to count extensive amounts of time. Knowing a great deal about the galaxy, they also were able to project the path of Earth as it moved through the vast reaches of space. By attuning to higher-dimensional wisdom, they learned that being in a certain location in the galaxy would impact Earth in a definable way.

The Mayans knew about the properties of energy fields and the vibratory waves found within them; and so they were able to gauge how the planet would be affected by its location in the galaxy. They possessed comprehensive knowledge of what it meant to be citizens of the universe and saw themselves as such. They knew that their role in the human family was to compile this information so that it could be used by future generations to understand the forces at work in their lives.

It is for this reason that a strong interest has surfaced in recent years regarding the Mayan people and their calendar. The Mayan calendar's current age of approximately five thousand years ends in

2012. This date has taken on a global significance as many are reflecting on the meaning of this end. They want to know how the planet and the people of Earth will be affected.

Some people are interpreting the end date of 2012 as catastrophic in nature. Others are exploring safe areas of the Earth to relocate if severe natural disasters destroy life as we know it on the planet. Many, however, have no interest in the Mayan predictions for the end of the age and are continuing as if there will be no impact on their lives in the foreseeable future.

We would like to acquaint you with what we see happening from a spiritual perspective as a vast cycle of time comes to a close. Although universal law gives free choice to incarnating souls on Earth, we can provide some general ideas about two specific forces that will be impacting life on your planet throughout the remainder of this century and beyond.

Transformation through Fire and Water

All continents and landmasses have entered into an extensive phase of physical transformation impulsed by the elements of fire and water. Those living upon Earth's surface are being impacted by these two forces, which are raising havoc with the topography of the planet. The element of fire is surfacing in the human condition through anger, strife, rage, conflict and war.

These incendiary states raise the vibratory levels found within the human body and increase the temperature levels found in all life on Earth's surface. We know that most people do not recognize the correlation between explosive feelings, which lead to conflict and war, and the primary element of fire; but they are directly related. Sorrow, grief and emotional pain are directly connected to the element of water.

Just as fire and water are bringing about the Great Purification in your physical environment, these same elements, in varying degrees, are impacting the behavior of those living on Earth's surface. It is very important to be consciously aware of the transformation underway and to embrace the positive aspects of it. In doing so, the children of Earth will utilize the maximum spiritual energies they will need to ascend the spiral of life.

Each human being has a soul reflecting the essence of the Creator of All That Is. This internal spark connects and attunes to the four primary forces, which were set in motion at the outset of creation to develop and guide life unfolding in all the universes of time, space and beyond. On the third-dimensional level, these forces are called earth, air, fire and water—terms used to closely reflect their mode of expression. Every aspect of life on your planet is activated and sustained by these four forces.

Earthquakes and the warming of Earth's temperatures are directly connected to the element of fire. This element is affecting the behavior of people in every area of the globe. How many times have you seen anger, rage and strife occurring in some aspect of your daily affairs? How quickly are interpersonal confrontations occurring between individuals or groups within your sphere of influence? Do you see these same kinds of behaviors at the national or international level? Wherever they surface, they are activated by the element of fire.

As the element of fire increases within the affairs of human beings on your planet, many seemingly detrimental occurrences will rise around the issue of fire, whether they are physical, emotional, psychological or spiritual. Earthquakes, volcanic upheavals, raging forest fires, military explosions and heating of the atmosphere all fall in the category of physical fire.

Emotions that heat up and bring forth anger, rage, and strife often result in harm to others, but particularly to those experiencing these states. The element of fire is found in these negative emotional states as well. The physical brain processing negative emotions is impacted by an increase in activity that stresses its neuropathways, causing an overheating at a molecular level.

Serenity is the natural state of the soul. When excessive fire is manifesting in a human being through the expression of turbulent, negative emotions, it can impact the soul far beyond what one would think. But fire can be expressed in positive ways on the levels we have named above. In the physical environment, fire often proves to have a cleansing and rejuvenating affect. In a mature forest, fire clears out old, dying trees to prepare the ground for new growth.

When an individual is able to conquer emotions of anger, fear, and hatred, that person's vibratory wavelength is raised, and a new level of human functioning is reached. The fire within hurtful emotions can increase the ability of incarnating souls to rise up the spiral of life if higher vibratory power is called upon to transform those emotions. So, you see, within the dualistic framework of your universe, everything has a positive and negative capability.

Fire always has been associated with spirituality since earliest times. Flames of all types have been part of ancient rituals throughout your planet. Fire increases the energy output of whatever it touches. Anger, rage and fear have vibratory wavelengths that heat and therefore expand. So do the spiritual practices of prayer and meditation.

In ancient India, the concept originated regarding the spiritual fire found coiled at the base of the spine, which when activated rises up to the crown of the head. It was called kundalini and was considered essential to the progress of the soul. When this spiritual fire reached the top of the head, enlightenment was attained, and a person became a realized being.

In other words, the individual achieved the knowledge that he or she is a child of God possessing an immortal soul on a journey of return to the Source from which it had come. Spiritual fire was the element bringing this state about. Therefore, we ask that you view an increase in the element of fire in your lives on all levels as an opportunity for spiritual growth. Wherever you encounter it, try to convert any negative expression into its higher spiritual counterpart—love and respect for all forms of life, no matter how they are manifesting.

The element of water is also one of the four primary forces in the universe responsible for evolutionary growth. Water on the physical level provides motion, fluidity, nurturance, cleansing and purification. Water is receptive, contains great power, can dissolve whatever is in its path in a slow inexorable way, and always seeks its lowest level. It can be a gentle, quiet pond, a swiftly flowing creek, or a river that moves with purpose towards its source of union—a lake or ocean. Water refreshes and nourishes whatever it touches.

Manifesting differently, water can unleash tremendous power, as seen in hurricanes, typhoons, tsunamis and snowstorms that bring flooding and wreak havoc all over the globe. Here the destructive aspect of water is brought into play when it destroys a given area so that new forms can emerge out of the wreckage of the old. Water also carries with it essential elements contributing to death and rebirth.

Whereas fire expands and heats up whatever it touches, water has a cooling and dissolving function that expresses itself quite differently from that of fire. When water and fire come together, they create steam, resulting in the combining of two different energy fields. Let us now look at how the ascendancy of the water element is impacting the inhabitants of Earth at the physical level.

Throughout Earth, excessive amounts of water or the lack thereof are primary conditions affecting many people. Drought conditions have been prevalent in some areas, while excessive flooding has forced people to flee their homes for safer ground. Sea levels are rising as the ice caps at the North and South Poles are melting during the planetary warming trend that has accelerated in recent decades.

Great storms gathering in the oceans of the world have fostered hurricanes and typhoons, which have brought large amounts of water inland, destroying homes, towns and cities with an accompanying loss of life and property. We realize that what we say here is recognized by those who live upon Earth's surface. What is not known, except perhaps by a few, is that the seemingly destructive effect of fire and water upon the planet is part of a spiritual plan to help humanity ascend up the spiral of life.

Earth exists within a universe created by a Divine Source of Intelligence. This Source has a spiritual plan and purpose for all its creation. The intent always has been to send out sparks from Source to move through many worlds to gain experience, knowledge and loving awareness of what it is to be a spiritual being moving through differing dimensions before returning to reunion with All That Is.

All life resonates to the intent of this Divine Plan. Everything that occurs is animated by a divinely positive purpose, no matter how negative it might appear. To incorporate this belief into the basic essence of one's world view will bring a sense of peace and harmony to what is occurring, whether it is positive or negative. Death and destruction clear the way for renewal and rebirth and have a constructive role in those experiences that cause pain and suffering.

The energetic properties of water are having an impact on not only physical and environmental levels, but also on human emotional and psychological states as well. Souls, who are currently incarnating on Earth, are experiencing a massive realignment of their emotional and psychological natures, which is being reflected on the physical level by excessive water conditions throughout the planet.

This process has been in effect for over a decade but presently is accelerating powerfully and transformatively in the affairs of human beings. Emotions are an important aspect of the human psyche. They provide richness and vibrancy to the human condition. Whenever emotions come into play, there is a heightened sense of connection that adds vivid color to every aspect of life.

In your universe, which is governed by the Law of Duality, powerful uplifting emotional states are counterbalanced by negative emotions that shred and destroy the sense of well-being. Emotions are always changing, shifting and transmuting into a different phase, just like the flow of water through a given area of land.

Emotions are rarely fixed and unchanging. They ebb and flow like the waters of a great ocean. Currently, the entire planet is cleansing and purifying itself emotionally and vibrationally. There is an energy field surrounding Earth that contains all emotional expressions held by those who have lived on the surface of the planet since it was created. It is this energy field that is being cleansed and purified.

As humanity prepares for a more highly advanced human species to appear, Gaia, the great being supplying the spiritual life force for your planet, is releasing all past emotions felt by those who have lived on Earth. This is triggering a corresponding emotional release by the incarnating souls on her surface, since it now is time to bring unity, harmony and balance into the emotional affairs of humanity.

In order for this goal to be reached, everyone needs to take responsibility for his or her expression of negative, hurtful emotions. Wherever anger, fear, rage, depression or any negative emotions are expressed, the surrounding energy field is lowered and adversely affected. In contrast, when love, respect and acceptance are released into any given situation, a higher vibrational state is achieved.

For this basic reason, all individuals on Earth need to see themselves as conductors of positive, spiritual energy. Whenever they feel themselves slipping into a negative emotional state, it is best to promptly halt the process and shift their mood into a more positive one. The release and transformation of inner negative emotions is one of the most important human activities needed on the planet today. The element of water is offering assistance and support for all those involved in this important transformation.

The Sacred Geometry of Numbers

All life revolves around the harmony of the spheres, which contains the sacred geometry of numbers. With this thought in mind, let us look at the year 2006, which reduces numerically to the single digit 8. Each of the numbers from 1 to 9 reflects an archetypal experience within all the spheres of God's creation, no matter how diverse.

Even though few are aware of it, the year 2006 served as a pivotal time for inhabitants of the third-dimensional Earth plane. In the future, many will look back and recognize that a shift of monumental proportions began during this period. Issues of peace versus war, love versus hate, and respect versus disrespect reached a turning point in the history of humankind.

On Earth, the number 8 relates to the consolidation of form found within every society or group. This consolidation ranges from the highest levels of government to the simplest family unit, which is a governing force in and of itself. At this time, human life on Earth requires the security of boundaries and structure implicit within the 8 vibration in order for growth and development to occur.

Whenever the divine number 8 is in ascendancy, these matters come up for emphasis. Eight is one of the nine primary numbers, which form the foundation for all that exists within every universe.

Each of the numbers from 1 to 9 emits a unique vibration, setting into motion a specific kind of creation whenever it is activated.

During the year 2006, the affairs of humans on your planet focused on societal groups, from government to organizations and families. In every situation, issues arose regarding the function of these structures. People all over Earth began to question the quality and effectiveness of the groups in which they found themselves. Ever so slowly, they began to realize that new ways had to be found, which were more humane, fair and balanced. Questions about values and beliefs became paramount in the affairs of individuals.

Many began to reflect upon and explore in depth the quality and purpose of their lives. They started to question the impact that government was having upon them. They looked at their work and wondered if it were enriching them at an emotional and spiritual level. They began also to view their family dynamics with a more discerning gaze. We cannot emphasize strongly enough what a valuable exercise this is.

The political events that surfaced in 2006 centered on the consolidation of power. In every area of life, either the positive aspects of power or its corresponding misuse seemed to be the order of the day. The positions of opposing political forces became more entrenched, which often resulted in the use of military action to enforce a certain ideological point of view.

Duality and polarity ruled in many areas of the globe, but even as this condition magnified, the faint light of a new day began to dawn. More and more people began to question basic assumptions about their responsibilities as citizens within their governmental structure, as well as their responsibility to Mother Earth and to all other inhabitants of the planet.

Ever so slowly, some began to turn away from conflict with those of opposing points of view. They began to realize that polarization and strife over a difference in values and outlook were counterproductive to the welfare of the whole. A glimmer of oneness as a prevailing attitude toward others began to appear in the minds and hearts of many.

Very often a shift of this magnitude starts at an inner level, hidden and barely recognized. It is like the rumbling of a volcano deep within the interior of Earth until it erupts with great power and force, entering the atmosphere for all to see. In a similar vein, human consciousness, which was activated in 2006 under the influence of the divine number 8, will expand and grow into a societal shift of major proportions in a later period of time.

Earth's Spiritual Blueprint

The time has come for incarnating souls on Earth to expand their view of themselves and the planet on which they live. Every form of life reduces down to a unit of energy with vibratory waves as the basis of that energy. So we ask you, our readers, to begin to think of yourselves in this context.

You consist of a mass of energetic particles and waves that have come together to form what you think of as your physical body on a three-dimensional level. The body you inhabit is a seemingly dense structure that actually is an open, constantly moving force field, which you think is solid. Nothing could be farther from the truth.

As you develop the ability to see with more discernment, you will begin to perceive humans as less dense. It will seem as if their physical reality is fading from your view. Not only will they become more difficult to see, they will emit a stronger light, reflecting their true essence. Eventually, the physical body will consist solely of particles of light.

At the present time, human beings who have the ability to see in this multidimensional fashion are said to have "sixth sight" or extrasensory perception. This is a capability that all inhabitants of your planet will possess in future centuries. Just think of the amazing times ahead. Many people will be able to see the colors of each other's energy fields or auras, as well as hear the sounds coming from realms never heard from before.

This is a brief glimpse of the profound advancement that will be occurring in human capabilities as you proceed on your evolutionary path back to union with your Creator. We want you to know that wondrous times and events lie ahead for those born in the future, but first the pain and suffering of previous centuries must be cleansed from Earth's planetary system.

All incarnating souls currently living on your planet have volunteered to participate in this Great Purification of which the native peoples have spoken for eons. We ask that you embrace the role you have chosen. You are tilling the fields of your planet and removing the weeds of negative human expression so that a brighter day can dawn on Earth—a day that will usher in a New Heaven and a New Earth.

We are asking that you face these challenges with the firm conviction that you are assisting a planetary shift of great magnitude. The human race is changing many of its basic values and assumptions about what constitutes a harmonious and balanced life. This shift will allow all incarnating souls to move toward the vision of a New World where love, respect, cooperation and harmony form the prevailing mores for all those living on your planet.

When this state is finally reached, Earth's powerful emissions of light will irradiate all life on a galactic level. We ask that you carry this knowing within your mind and heart. Let it uphold and sustain you as you work in the vineyards of Earth producing a garden of great beauty. Never forget that all life is interconnected, and even the smallest act of consciousness-raising brings transformation beyond what you can envision.

The soul, an individualized unit of spirit, has embarked upon a long and arduous journey back to reunion with the Creator of All That Is. The experiences in this process propel the soul ever onward up the spiral of life. At key junctures, intense periods in life arise to provide a fertile field for soul growth. Earth during the twentieth and twenty-first centuries was, and is, in the throes of just such an expansion.

The issues of conflict, strife, war and death are surfacing on a worldwide scale unprecedented in earlier times. Warfare has served as a catalyst for humanity's accelerated growth and development. It is necessary for this old paradigm on Earth to be shattered in order for a new human expression to emerge. War has always been one of the major ways in which great societal change occurs. People's daily lives are disrupted and rarely return to the way they were before the conflict began.

When one sees an area that has been devastated by the conflict of war, it is clear that what existed previously has been eliminated and changed forever. We do not want to give the impression that these changes are always negative in nature. Often, outdated and obsolete ways of living are removed so that a new form of existence can emerge—one more conducive to spiritual growth and development. This has been the unfolding evolutionary pattern on Earth for millennia.

But a new day is dawning. The light of spirit is spreading slowly but surely throughout the globe. A time will come in which a more advanced way to live will be reached without pain and suffering. People will be able to recognize that their current cycle of experience is ending, and that it is now time to receive a new series of life situations more suitable to a higher form of functioning.

Just think of the massive shift this new approach will bring. At first, only a few will have the ability to move into an expanded state of consciousness, gained without the struggle and pain of war to clear the slate for a fresh start. But gradually this ability will spread, as more and more individuals attune to their inner soul wisdom and shift their values and beliefs to a higher level.

Once the inhabitants of your planet reach this place in their inner growth and development, the spiritual irradiation emitting from Earth will increase a thousand-fold. It is for this purpose that your planet was created by the Source of All That Is. The spiritual blueprint for Earth was one where matter was crystallized into its densest form. Human beings then would be the generators of spiritual development for the planet through a long progression of many lifetimes of trial and error.

Eventually the deepest point of descent into matter would be reached, and the journey back to Spirit would begin. This is where the inhabitants of Earth are now. The corner has been turned. Those living at the present time are helping to establish the shift in consciousness, which is bringing about a reunion with the Source of All That Is. To change the way something progresses, an extensive output of energy is necessary in order to stop a given course and turn it in a totally new direction.

Inertia is very strong in something that has existed for a long time. It takes great energy to accomplish a change in direction. It is for this reason that all areas of life have become so intense. It requires great force to begin this upward ascent. Mundane events have taken on a magnitude of importance unseen in earlier times. Because of technological advancements, individuals throughout the planet can experience simultaneously events of great importance unfolding daily.

As people attune and respond to the massive societal changes occurring in every corner of the globe, their inner spirit is activated and projected out into the ethers surrounding Earth. The energy field accompanying this projection carries with it the force necessary to break through the inertia of the old ways and shift humankind's course to a higher evolutionary level.

We ask you to take these words into your minds and hearts. Feel the power of what is said here. Every time you discard an old way of thinking and replace it with a more enlightened view, you have contributed to the spiritual development of your species. As the people of your planet reach a state of interconnectedness, unity and love, a New Heaven and a New Earth will begin to emerge. Can you not feel the desire for change rising within you? Follow your inner sense and join in the creative process. Is it not a wondrous time in which to live?

CHAPTER 5

Transformation of the Human Race

Recognition of the existence of the soul will be one of the foremost advances made by human beings in the next two hundred years on your planet. In the earliest times on Earth, souls forgot from whence they had come and related primarily to the material world around them. They forgot that they had been sent on a journey by God to grow and experience many realms of existence in order to reflect back the realities of creation. The forgetting, however, was necessary for their spiritual growth. Expanded consciousness is best realized when something of great importance is missing and must be found to achieve wholeness.

And so it is that incarnating souls on Earth have hardwired into their DNA a divine discontent that spurs them on to ever greater exploration of who they are and why they are here. This quality guarantees the continuation of an evolutionary process that never is forgotten at the soul level. Even in the quietest phases of human development when soul progress seems stalled, a percolation of spiritual energy is occurring, stimulating a return to spiritual advancement at some point.

The universe occupied by Earth's solar system has been in an expanding mode for eons. Every aspect of life has been moving away from the center that contains the Source of All That Is. At a given moment, however, the outward motion will stop and reverse its course, bringing all life back to its place of original creation. This process of expansion and contraction clearly reflects the theme of duality established by the Creator at the outset of the current period of manifestation.

Why is this information significant to the journey of the soul? Every incarnating soul needs to see its role in the divine flow of life. It is only through contact with the inner essence of spirit that the recognition of this role occurs. Until soul contact is made on a continuous basis, knowledge and understanding of an individual's true purpose in life cannot be reached.

How is this continuous contact achieved, you may ask? The answer is surprisingly simple. By closing one's eyes, breathing deeply and rhythmically, and entering into the inner stillness, attunement to the higher self occurs. This process is currently called meditation and opens the pathway for interaction with the soul. It is in this inner space of calm and peace between thoughts that the soul communicates its wisdom and love, guiding us homeward to eventual union with the Creator of All That Is.

Expansion of the Human Brain

The journey human beings are taking has significance far beyond that envisioned by most individuals. Information regarding the existence of the soul and the realms of spirit is beginning to enter the consciousness of those incarnating on the Earth plane at the present time. This knowledge will have a major impact on human evolution and will prepare the way for a more advanced species waiting to incarnate.

This new prototype of human being will have an expanded brain capacity beyond what is found in today's inhabitants of your planet. New pathways in the brain will be needed to register interaction with beings from other dimensions at a conscious level. In order for this communication to happen, there has to be clear recognition of the process that is unfolding.

Since the brain initiates all thought and action, the full complement of synapses creating mental activity must be operational in order to reflect the new experiences of Earth's inhabitants. So it is that one of the most significant advances made in human development in the next two centuries will be this expansion of brain capacity.

This is why there has been so much emphasis on the development of the left hemisphere of the brain during the past three hundred years on Earth. Both the right and left hemispheres of the brain must be fully functional in order for the next important step in human evolution to begin.

For those of you who chafe within a societal structure that places such emphasis on intellectual achievement, we ask you to recognize the necessity for this development. The human brain must balance the opposite but complimentary functions of the right and left hemispheres. By the beginning of the twenty-first century, that goal was reached. The human brain is now ready to master the realm of matter.

The physical brain serves as the conductor and regulator of all activity originated by the higher mind. In order for more advanced realities to be reflected, the physical brain must expand its functioning to recognize unfamiliar situations as they unfold within the human condition. In the future, multidimensional travel by the physical body will become more common. As incarnating souls on your planet travel into higher dimensions, the human brain must be equipped to reflect what is happening on many different levels simultaneously.

In the past one thousand years, physical bodies of the planet's inhabitants have been steadily growing larger, particularly in the area of the head. This bigger head size, occurring more and more often in newborns, is a necessary development in the evolution of the human race. As the brain increases in operational complexity, the head encasing it must grow to accommodate the expansion. This change provides an outward indication of the great advance underway on your planet.

Realigning DNA

During this present age on Earth, a vast group of humanity is moving onto the threshold of a higher dimension. The time of preparation has come to an end, and the ascension to a higher plane of reality is about to begin. For eons, incarnating souls have come to your planet knowing that they were to be workers in the vineyards, preparing the way for a major evolutionary step to occur in the distant future.

The time for that step has finally arrived, and a significant step in the evolution of the human race is coming, slowly but surely. At key intervals in the history of Earth, the developmental path of humanity has been accelerated by a stimulation of the human DNA. This genetic code was put in place within the human body to regulate and upgrade the physical structure when the time for human transformation arrived.

Many things have modified the human DNA. At times, energy fields emanating from the center of the galaxy directed impulses that changed the human body. At other times, the planet herself emitted a frequency from deep within her core that modified DNA in a wide variety of ways. And upon a few occasions, beings from other star systems manipulated human DNA in order to accelerate the evolutionary process.

In recent years, there has been a burgeoning interest in the role that DNA has played in the development of the human race. The scientific and medical fields have honed in on the whole area of DNA in relation to health and heredity. Cures are being found for illnesses by accessing the genetic code and revising its molecular structure to eliminate weaknesses creating specific areas of ill health.

As more is discovered about the significance of DNA, the basic building block of life, a scientific field will emerge centered on improving the physical and mental capabilities of human beings. A change in DNA is needed so that the human race can develop the expanded capabilities required for the next great evolutionary step.

These higher capabilities cannot appear in the human body and mind as it is presently constituted. A dramatic realignment of the current DNA must take place to create a body of greater size and strength with a brain capacity that will accommodate a wide variety of extrasensory skills and abilities. In order for this improvement in human functioning to occur, the DNA must go through a restructuring and change from its present state.

The Coming Shift in Perception

It is time for the children of Earth to step back, take a deep breath and look at themselves and their lives. The vast majority of human activity emanates from habitual behavior and rote memory. Very little originates from a new and creative way of viewing life. Most individuals perpetuate the status quo by repeating over and over again what is familiar and therefore comfortable.

Some people will not agree with what we have said here. There is the common misperception among many that they are having varied and unusual experiences during their daily lives. If one were to reflect more deeply on the events filling the course of each day, it would slowly become evident that the same types of activity are being repeated with perpetual regularity.

To illustrate what we are saying here, let us take a day in the life of a hypothetical person. If the individual is an adult, more than likely certain activities form the core of what is done each day. Work, eating, sleeping and some type of relaxation are primary. These four categories comprise the bulk of any twenty-four hour period.

The amount of time given to each of these four categories can vary, but the categories themselves generally do not change. We are speaking of this issue now because your planet soon will be moving into an energy field that will modify the way life is lived on Earth. No longer will the security of habitually repetitive behavior characterize human existence.

It will become imperative that those living in the future on Earth include creativity and spontaneity in every aspect of their lives. The vibratory makeup of the human body is in the process of changing. All physical matter will become less dense and this will require that life be lived in a complimentary balance with the energy field in which it resides.

The molecular waves found in all physical existence will be vibrating faster than they do now. This increased rate of movement will break up crystallization of any form. Creativity, flexibility, spontaneity and originality will be needed in order to bring a New World into being. Those who rigidly adhere to the old ways of living will be unable to participate in the momentous change occurring in all walks of life.

As severe weather conditions impact and reconfigure land masses all over the globe, people will have to find new places and means of existence. When familiar societal structures break apart, they will have to be replaced with new forms that are more suitable in a world that barely resembles the one existing before.

Being able to change course and move in a new direction will be necessary in the centuries ahead. The rigidity of living within constantly repeated behavioral patterns will be detrimental to all levels of continued existence. The ability to intuitively sense and anticipate what is coming will become increasingly important for human survival.

Much is unfolding in the universes of the Creator at this point in the evolutionary development of all life. The period of great expansion over the eons is beginning to slow and is changing its momentum to reflect the reversal in course, long anticipated by the highest initiates down through the ages.

Wise individuals have been innately aware of the developmental path created by the Source of All That Is. They have known that all life was moving away from the Source of Creation. They also have known that at a certain point this outer movement would stop and reverse itself, beginning the arduous return to the center of each universe where the point of creation began.

This knowledge has been held in key locations throughout the many universes of time and space. It has been kept alive in sacred scriptures that are generally unavailable. It is a body of esoteric thought little known or understood. On Earth, the awareness of these universal energies has been held in trust by loyal individuals down through the ages.

Those who have kept this information intact have had a wide variety of names. We shall refer to them as Keepers of the Flame. The element of fire has always been associated with the many aspects of spirit. And so it is that those Keepers of the Flame have passed on this knowledge in an unbroken chain since the beginnings of sentient life on your planet.

Even though awareness of this knowledge has seemed to disappear at various times during the history of humankind, it has never been lost. It has just gone underground, as you would say, to emerge at a later date when circumstances were more auspicious. Periods of great light and advancement are often followed by times of darkness and seeming loss of momentum. In reality, this is not a loss of forward motion. It is just a cessation of movement in order to provide renewal and regeneration during the long evolutionary journey back to Source.

You may wonder what relevance this abstract information can have for the average person living on Earth at this time. We assure you that understanding the basic motion of your solar system within its galaxy and then its universe is critical at this time. Humanity is moving up the spiral of life. From this vantage point, many will begin to see that they are units of energy swimming in a molecular mass of vibratory particles and waves emanating from the center of your galaxy.

As people incorporate this realization into their world view at the deepest level of comprehension, a monumental shift in perception will occur. To see in such a new and revolutionary way will create an awareness that will catapult them into a more advanced phase of evolution. They will not be able to continue to operate within a three-dimensional frame of mind.

Many will begin to see the undulating waves of subatomic particles that constitute the background for all life. As the ability to witness energy in its purest form continues to develop in human beings, great advancements will occur in all areas of life. The primordial building blocks of life found throughout the universe will come to be used as the underlying creative source for all that is manifested.

Slowly, more and more incarnating souls will tune into the quality of energy swirling about them. They will start, ever so faintly, to feel the universal pulsation that underlies all life on every dimensional level. This ever-present throbbing movement forms the background for every thing that exists in the many universes of time and space.

This pulsation constitutes the primordial emanation from the Source of All That Is at the moment of creation. In the many pictures taken of deep space, it is the darkness against which every aspect of existence is reflected. This background receives little attention from astronomers in their study of the heavens as they try to identify the origin of stars, comets, planets, solar systems and galaxies.

Once it is found that the dark, undulating backdrop for all stellar life is made up of the energy released at the beginning of creation, humankind will begin to identify and understand the nature of God. In the Hindu tradition, this vast energy field is called Shakti, the creative force of the universe. It has a two-fold movement, expansion and contraction.

When the first breath of life emanated from the mind of God, it moved out from its Source in ever-widening concentric circles. These circles took on the form of undulating waves of creative energy that gathered force and momentum as they progressed. Everything within this field operates from a basic premise of expansion and contraction. It is the core principle for life on every level of existence.

The knowledge that each experience in life will be activated and motivated by a desire to grow and expand will provide an important awareness for the incarnating soul. There will be an understanding that forward movement is the basic dynamic for all life, no matter what its form. Once this principle is understood, creative expression of any kind can be realized just by attuning to and merging with the underlying energy of the universe.

The Subconscious Mind

Now we would like to explore in depth the nature of the subconscious mind. During the past one hundred and fifty years, there has been a reawakening of interest, study and research in the field of psychology regarding the existence and nature of the subconscious mind. This interest marks an important step in the soul's evolutionary journey.

Every incarnating individual has a construct of three mental forces—the subconscious, the conscious and the super-conscious minds. These three forms are always functioning and interrelating in every aspect of human existence. At this time on Earth, only one mental construct is recognized and used by the vast majority of people throughout the planet, that of the conscious mind.

All developed forms of life operate within a force field of three, which is why most major religious traditions honor the importance of the number three. The power of the mental force separates human beings on Earth from the lower forms of life. The mind operating within the physical brain provides the bridge for more advanced spiritual progress.

During the past five hundred years on Earth, the focus has been on developing and refining the conscious mind with its many attributes. Science has been the primary vehicle for the necessary emphasis and training. To assist soul growth, it has been necessary to gain maximum utilization of the conscious mind as it exists within its mental framework.

A developed conscious mind is a needed tool to assist the coming evolutionary step on your planet. It is for this reason that the growth of intellectual capabilities has received such attention and priority status in the educational process. In the twenty-first century, with its primary theme of unity, the interconnection of the subconscious, the super-conscious, and the conscious minds will be better understood.

The two great pioneers of psychology, Sigmund Freud and Carl Jung, were responsible for opening the doors of awareness to the existence of the subconscious mind; but their work only begins to tap the power of this great reservoir of the soul. The subconscious mind holds an individual's experiences, thoughts and emotions at a level of unawareness, to be released at a specific time and under a certain set of circumstances.

Each soul comes into incarnation with subconscious memories, which are an accumulation of various life experiences from every level of existence. These memories form a record of the soul's journey through the many dimensions of time and space. They are a body of knowledge that can be accessed whenever needed. They are a testimony to the ongoing journey of the soul.

As the inhabitants of your planet shift more and more into a new realm of consciousness, recognizing the existence of the subconscious mind will become more prevalent. Incarnating souls will learn how to access the knowledge and wisdom stored in the subconscious mind as part of everyday living.

The subconscious holds the memory of all that has been learned while moving through the fields of matter. It also contains memories of experiences in other realms throughout the universe. It is intended that this knowledge be held within the matrix of the soul until the final reunion with Source occurs. The long journey of the soul is meant, in part, to provide the Creator of All That Is with the awareness of what it is to live within its own creation.

So it is that the memory bank of the subconscious serves as a vital reservoir of information, which can provide valuable insights into human life. We mean this in a very practical and mundane way. Let us provide some examples to aid you in grasping the role the subconscious mind plays in all areas of life. One example might be found within a context familiar to many—that of driving on today's roads and freeways.

Very often incidents will occur where motorists impinge on someone else's lane or space, sometimes causing serious accidents or death. For those who survive these events, there can be, at times, a post-traumatic stress reaction totally out of proportion to what has happened. This response occurs because the subconscious mind has released feelings from other instances in which the individual was almost killed or injured.

Most people do not recognize the depth of pain that surfaces when a loved one dies. They do not realize that the sorrow of deaths from this or other lifetimes surfaces as they contend with the loss of this loved one. In earlier times, the necessity for a year of grieving and removal from many aspects of life was the norm. People knew at a subliminal level that the recovery process took time and much effort to heal.

Since the loss of a loved one activates other losses, one is dealing with many layers of emotional distress. What a difference it would make if one accepted the process as an opportunity to heal the pain of death at a much deeper level. It is also a great help if one knows that each person has an eternal soul which never dies, and that the loved one still exists in another form and place.

Knowingly retrieving information from the subconscious mind helps expand human awareness regarding the true nature of the soul. Every person in human form possesses not only a physical body but also this tripartite mind force, which increases awareness until the state of consciousness is reached where reunion with the Almighty is possible.

The Milky Way Galaxy—A Matrix for Life

Life is like a kaleidoscope of many different colors that are shifting and refracting back a multiplicity of hues and shapes. Another analogy for life is the merry-go-round or carousel that moves in a never-ending circle around a fixed pole. One of the basic laws of the universe is based on circular motion.

Solar systems, galaxies, and universes revolve in a circular pattern around a center of great power and force. This circular motion often assumes the form of a spiral, which always moves upward with every turn of the circle. The spiral is the most accurate form describing the evolutionary journey of the soul.

The soul progresses through a wide variety of experiences in many different realms of existence. The soul's true purpose is to gain knowledge of what it means to be a child of God moving through the varying levels of creation. As the soul proceeds on its journey through time, space, and beyond, it moves up the spiral of life, repeating certain experiences on ever more advanced levels until the highest point in the spiral has been reached.

At the pinnacle, a profound understanding is gained regarding a particular kind of life lesson that has been repeated until mastery is achieved. The soul then leaves the circular repetition of that particular spiral and moves to one containing a different but equally important series of lives addressing a new area of spiritual growth and development. We have just given you a brief picture describing the evolutionary path of the soul.

For eons, the spiral has been a sacred symbol. It can be found in the earliest cave drawings of prehistoric humans. Over and over, it has been etched on rock walls all over the planet. Even more ancient spirals have been discovered in excavations deep below the surface. There has been much conjecture by archeologists and anthropologists as to the meaning of the many spirals they encounter.

Those who study the spirals on rock walls assume that there must be some important significance to them, because they appear so often. They are simply a description of the path that the soul takes on its journey through creation. They were drawn and carved to remind human beings of their spiritual origins and the passage they are taking to reunite with their Creator.

Indigenous peoples have carried forward the importance of circular movement by incorporating it into dance and spinning rituals. They perform this movement to keep reminding themselves of their spiritual origins and journey as they return to Great Spirit. They also know, even though it may not be consciously, that they are bringing in a power that uplifts them on many different levels.

Monumental changes will be occurring in human physiology as the energy field of Earth moves up to a higher vibratory level. Impulses from the center of your galaxy are impacting your planet with increasing regularity. Every time this happens, the vibratory field of all sentient life makes a slight but discernable shift in its molecular structure. More human beings can tell that something unseen is affecting them at many different levels. They sense that they are changing physically, emotionally and psychologically, though they do not know the cause or source of this alteration.

It is now time for incarnating souls on your planet to recognize that they live within a galactic field that serves as the font of energy for all that exists within it. Inhabitants of Earth see the locale where they reside and other areas of the planet where they may travel as the boundaries of their existence. This view is truly limiting to spiritual growth and development and is far from the truth of what the totality of life is for them.

One of the greatest advancements in human evolution during this current millennium will be the growing recognition that the Milky Way Galaxy has provided the womb for all life on Earth. Your planet is an integral part of the galaxy's spiritual journey as it travels through a certain area of your universe. The deeper significance of this concept will become more widely understood in coming centuries.

If this awareness is not attained, humanity will remain fixed within a three-dimensional reality, which will prevent a new species with more advanced capabilities from incarnating on Earth. It is imperative that the people of your planet begin to expand the concept of who you really are. You live within a unified field of continuously widening vibratory waves.

Anything that occurs within your universe touches you like the faint whispering of ever-blowing winds. You are connected energetically to all forms of life found in your universe. This is the reality of the unified field. Every form of life in the universe is joined to every other form in a subtle dance of waves and particles. Humanity needs to accept this view of reality in order for the next great evolutionary step to be taken.

Therefore, when you feel an unidentifiable sensation with no evident reason for its existence, know that a vibratory shift is occurring somewhere within the galactic field, making a subtle impact on the life of your planet. Accept it and recognize that it is instrumental in helping you progress. In the centuries to come, those living on Earth will be able to recognize changes in the energy emanating from the center of your galaxy as easily as weather is predicted on your planet at the present time.

CHAPTER 6

Fear and Trust

Time is short, and there is urgency in the affairs of humans on the Earth plane. Many on the level of spirit are sending information in a variety of forms to your planet to assist in the great transformation that is underway. As we have said before, your third-dimensional realm of dense matter is experiencing a massive purification at all levels.

This cleansing is removing the debris that has accumulated for eons in all areas of life. Physically and environmentally, land throughout the globe is being impacted by severe weather conditions altering the topography of Earth. These developments are awakening people to the fact that powerful events are changing their lives in profound ways.

Long-held values are being questioned, making it appear that the very fabric of society is eroding. The physical health of many incarnating on Earth is being affected in a detrimental way by pollution and worsening air quality, particularly in industrial nations. People are turning to their religious beliefs in an attempt to understand and cope with the many adversities affecting humanity at the present time.

All of these seemingly negative conditions are providing fertile ground for the emergence of a new human species and the world that it will inhabit. As gardeners know, before planting a new crop the weeds must be removed, the ground tilled, and nutrients added in order to insure a bountiful yield. Everything that is unfolding on Earth at the present time is analogous to preparing the soil for new growth.

The destructive aspects of life found in the human condition need to be brought forward and eradicated just as weeds need to be removed before planting. What are these destructive aspects, you may ask? In essence, they can be found in the lack of respect and in the hurtful thoughts, words or actions between individuals, groups or nations that have existed on your planet throughout the centuries.

Even though there have been periods on Earth where the light of spirit has shone in the past, by and large the story of humanity has been one of conflict, strife and warfare. From the time when the first primitive hominid picked up a bone to use as a weapon to the current period where nuclear weapons threaten the very quality of life, it has been considered acceptable to hurt, maim or kill other human beings for a wide variety of reasons.

The seeds of death and destruction have been sown by many cultures down through the ages. War has been glorified as a legitimate means for gaining supremacy over others. The sanctity of human life has been undervalued and ignored as power and domination have prevailed in many countries. These are the weeds that need to be eradicated from the human garden, and now is the time.

Along with the ravages of warfare, the state of the planet is of growing concern all over the globe. It has taken an extended period of time for a majority of people to recognize that Earth is going through a dramatic change in weather and is experiencing catastrophic climate conditions unlike anything seen in recorded history.

As destructive earthquakes, tornadoes, hurricanes, tsunamis and droughts increase in number and severity, their impact is awakening people in every walk of life. All levels of society are beginning to recognize that something monumental is unfolding. Older people can attest to the fact that the weather has become much more severe than anything they experienced in their early years.

Since the news media feature climatic events as they unfold, there is instant viewing of catastrophic weather occurring at any locale on the planet. The modern technology of television makes it possible to see an event and experience its magnitude without actually being there. These pictures produce a powerful visual imprint, affecting the viewer at a far deeper level than can be imagined.

Fearfulness and anxiety are becoming more pronounced as one severe weather episode follows another. Climate change and warming of the planet are rising to the top of concerns expressed by many, producing a global awareness as nations and key individuals meet to discuss and seek solutions to the problem.

We ask that you look at this situation from a higher spiritual perspective. As we have said before, your Mother Earth is experiencing an increase in her vibratory rate in order to irradiate her energy field in preparation for the new human species coming into incarnation. Part of this process requires an expansion of outlook for those who walk on her surface.

Human culture has evolved from individual and group survival to identification with tribe, town, city, state, and nation over many eons on your planet. For brief periods in the far distant past, a global consciousness existed on your planet in places where there remains no record. All life on Earth cycles and recycles, presenting recurring themes as humanity progresses towards ever higher states of consciousness.

In the distant future, the inhabitants of Earth will develop a state of interconnectedness with all forms of life on the planet. This will be achieved through many cycles of trial and error. At the present time, a new period of global interaction is emerging. The growing worldwide awareness regarding increasingly intense climate changes is bringing this concern into manifestation.

Letting Go of Fear

For those living on the Earth plane, experiencing a higher dimension requires modifying the rate at which one's force field is vibrating within a given space. The various realms or dimensions are interwoven in a vast web of molecular waves and particles. These dimensions have different vibratory velocities, which require anyone entering that spatial construct to be vibrating at the same rate.

It is very important to understand the concept of molecular movement. One of the major developments of this current millennium will be the human ability to engage in multidimensional travel. In order for the process to begin, it will be necessary to believe that other dimensions exist and that accessing them is a part of the birthright of all life. Once this certainty grows, it takes on an urgency that will not be quelled until the journey of exploration begins.

The first step in expanding consciousness to the point where one enters other dimensions requires a strong mental intent to initiate the process. One needs to expand one's awareness of what life is really about and to release all fear of the consequences. Fear is a constricting force prohibiting forward movement of any kind.

Expansion can never occur when any type of contraction exists at the physical, emotional, psychological or spiritual level. Therefore a person must remove fear at any of these levels before multidimensional travel can occur. This can be done by conducting a thorough inventory of any element of the individual's life that causes one to resist or to stop and withdraw. Aversion is generally a sign that fear exists at the core of that experience.

Once one has identified an area where resistance or aversion exists, a clear look at the cause must occur for the process of healing to begin. The next step requires forming a strong intent to remove and release the mental and emotional elements of the fear, which is creating a paralysis of sorts. When this point is reached, the negative effect of the fear will dissipate and finally disappear.

We cannot emphasize strongly enough the importance of identifying whenever fears constrict or prevent one from achieving a state of well-being. Apprehension of any kind hinders evolutionary progress for the incarnating soul. It lowers the vibratory rate, which then in turn inhibits the natural tendency to ascend the spiral of life.

The single most important challenge facing those currently living on Earth is to identify, address and heal any area of life containing the element of fear. It is the greatest impediment to the growth and development of the soul. For this reason, fear and its corresponding state of worry must be removed from the human condition.

Two important issues facing humanity on Earth during the current millennium will be the discontinuance of war as a means of settling disputes and the eradication of fear within the human psyche. We have indicated the impact fear has upon an individual and how it impedes forward motion. It prohibits the ability to initiate significant steps needed for the growth and development of the soul.

Much time and effort has been spent on various techniques and methods intended to eliminate a wide variety of fears. We would like to offer our thoughts with some aspects that are used currently by psychologists, therapists or counselors on how to address this long-standing emotional weakness. We believe that certain actions, if thoroughly and diligently embarked upon, can conquer this negative condition.

The first step is to identify clearly and completely the fear that needs to be removed. It is necessary to look at the fear, describe in detail what causes it and recognize the effect it has on the individual. All elements connected to the fear must be brought into conscious awareness for the process of removal to begin. The person experiencing the fear needs to own and fully understand the fear.

Once that process of identification and understanding has been completed, the next level involving removal of the fear can begin. However, the individual must be dedicated to the goal of removing the fear permanently. The mental power of strong intent must be activated, accompanied by a firm and unshakable resolve. Only if the individual is willing to do this will the effort bring the desired results.

When this state has been reached, the individual needs to produce a positive statement regarding the elimination of the fear. For instance, the statement might be, "I am safe and secure whenever I am in the dark." This affirmation needs to be said over and over, internally or externally, to reprogram the subconscious mind.

The person working on eliminating fear must gather the strength of will and inner resolve to conquer this negative emotion. If he or she cannot do so, then the process must be postponed until there is a strong enough motivation and intent to deal with the problem. This process is of great value since it not only removes a debilitating emotion, but it also starts to train the individual in the Law of Manifestation, a most important capability for the evolving soul.

After conscientiously repeating positive affirmations for a given period of time decided on by the individual, a test of the fear should be tried. The degree of difficulty can be determined by the person or with someone who is assisting in the process. If the fear is diminishing, the test will be successful and will provide the confidence needed to proceed to a higher level of difficulty. This process needs repeating until the fear is removed.

The value in this method is that it involves the total commitment and participation of the person experiencing the fear. He or she is the one who solves and eliminates the problem—not another person doing it. Healing of self is the desired end result, since fear always contains a loss of personal power. Therefore, the most effective mode for eradicating fear or any other emotional weakness rests in the person himself or herself accomplishing the healing. Only through this means will the individual regain the will and ability to overcome this incapacitating condition.

Developing Trust

The ability to trust needs to be attained by all incarnating souls on the Earth plane. Trust will be sorely needed in the years ahead. Trust involves having a positive view of life, even though circumstances may indicate otherwise. Trust is a difficult state to reach, particularly if an individual has experienced situations that have destroyed the capacity to think affirmatively about one's self or some area of one's life.

Trust is founded on certainty and conviction, helped by awareness that there is a powerful force for good unfolding in life. This belief allows one to develop the ability to face trials, no matter how difficult and painful. Also, trust often activates the Law of Manifestation, ultimately creating the very result for which the trust was needed.

Fear and lack of trust are the prevailing emotional states in the world at this time. Energetically they are reflected as darkness in the human body's force field, which prevents the free flow of life force. In the future, human beings will be able to see the auras around themselves and others and will be able to identify the darkness, its corresponding obstruction of energy flow, and its cause.

Until this capability is developed in most of the incarnating souls on Earth, it will be necessary to identify trust or fear through a scrupulous inventory of one's emotions, thoughts and actions. Only by emulating the clear and piercing gaze of the eagle can you bring trust into conscious awareness.

Later in the twenty-first century, there will be much turmoil, change and disruption. In order to deal with these conditions, it will be necessary to function from a state of detachment and trust, with the conviction that all is in divine order and contributing to the spiritual evolution of the human race. When one has achieved this state, it will be possible to function as a world server—an individual who can bring help and healing to others.

During this century, healing will become one of the highest priorities in people's lives. It will involve healing of the planet, the environment, and society on every level of existence. As people become aware of powerful forces of negativity, they will begin to focus more and more on eradicating them. The ability to trust will be needed to accomplish this essential shift in planetary awareness.

This is a time of profound transformation for incarnating souls on the Earth plane. Time is speeding up, and the affairs of human beings are accelerating in urgency and intensity. The established order of things is being shaken at its core, and change in many areas of life has become the norm. Because so much in life has been altered in one way or another, a low-level state of anxiety can be found in many individuals.

Free-floating anxiety is the cause of a variety of ills that are currently surfacing all over the planet. Anxiety causes nervous tension, which in turn results in psychological, emotional and physical ailments. The entire body becomes strained and out of balance when the anxious person is overtaken by apprehension, concern and worry.

As Earth enters a period of intense change and readjustment, daily affairs become stretched beyond accustomed parameters. For many people, being forced beyond one's comfort zone is a stressful and upsetting experience. Security is a basic need, since most human beings want to live within an established system that is reliable and dependable. Familiarity brings a sense of comfort and continuity within which an individual can find refuge and relax.

When the status quo is threatened or disrupted, various levels of anxiety set in for many people. Equilibrium is disturbed, and they fall into an imbalanced condition. Anxiety can cause headaches, heart palpitations, digestive disorders or a wide variety of other physical symptoms. On an emotional level, depression, volatile mood swings, exhaustion or hopelessness can arise.

For these reasons, we ask that you fearlessly scrutinize your psychological and emotional state of mind. Identify whether you are apprehensive or worried about anything in your life. If so, then our information may be helpful for you. Anxiety can be eliminated by changing the way you look at what is upsetting you, if you can reach that state of mind.

In order to alter your reaction to what is causing concern in your life, you must be willing to develop trust regarding all that is, or may be, affecting you adversely. If you can come to believe that everything which happens is for your highest good and will enhance your spiritual growth and development, you will gain a sense of equanimity and trust about all you are facing.

Faith and conviction in the rightness of what is unfolding in life is the true outlook of the spiritually enlightened person. Anxiety can never take hold when this view of life is held. How does one achieve this confidence and conviction? It happens by attuning to your own inner wisdom through meditation, prayer or other spiritual practices that raise your vibratory rate and bring you into contact with your soul essence. Your soul knows that everything is ultimately for the highest good. Gaining this knowledge will support you through whatever happens. Trust in this and all will be well!

CHAPTER 7

A Shift in Time

All life on Earth is in a process of acceleration. For many, time seems to have speeded up in a noticeable way. And truly this is the case. Time was established by the Creator to be a form of measurement in the affairs of incarnating souls living on the Earth plane. It provided a structure within which the unfolding of daily occurrences was reflected. With its past, present and future overlay, time gave a backdrop for the human condition. It appeared to be a constant that could be relied upon.

But time no longer is a reliable measurement of human affairs, because time, as the inhabitants of Earth know it, is moving faster now. It no longer can be viewed as a steady progression of events for those living on your planet. Time ebbs and flows like a vast ocean in a primordial sea. Periodically, it slows its momentum, providing various life forms an opportunity to assimilate evolutionary vibratory waves coming from the center of the universe.

Everything exists at a basic level in wavelike form, undulating throughout time and space. These waves have a rhythm that speeds up or slows down depending on the Creator's intent. Throughout a period of acceleration, spiritual growth causes the soul to move to a higher level on its evolutionary spiral. New knowledge and profound insights come to all life forms during this phase.

In these periods, time moves more rapidly. Presently, all life on planet Earth is experiencing this increase in time's wavelike motion. Every aspect of life is being speeded up, creating intensity in situations that previously moved at a more leisurely pace. To test the accuracy of what we have said here, we ask you to look back at how you were living fifteen years ago and compare that period with today.

Did life back then seem simpler, less complicated or moving at a slower pace than now? Do you currently feel under pressure to accomplish tasks within the time you have allotted for them? If so, then you are attuning to the universal rhythms moving throughout Earth's force field. One of the most important steps in the journey of the soul is the ability to consciously recognize planetary and universal energies and incorporate them into daily living.

Time is entering a heightened state for the inhabitants of Earth. A powerful shift in consciousness is underway. The very concept of time is changing. For eons on your planet, time has been seen from a linear perspective, which categorized it within the framework of past, present and future. This view of time is beginning to change dramatically because of discoveries being made in the field of physics.

The emergence of a new scientific paradigm, quantum physics, is reflecting time and reality in an entirely new and different way. Its basic premise is that life exists in an energetic field, which is always changing and transforming according to the stimuli being applied to that field. Therefore, reality is not as it appears to those living within the third dimension of Earth.

Time is one of the basic cornerstones of life on your planet. As more and more people on Earth gain the ability to move into multidimensional consciousness, they will experience time in a far different way than they do now. Life in the many dimensions of the Creator unfolds in a variety of settings, offering diversity for the evolving soul.

For this reason, the soul always is seeking the circumstances most suitable for its growth. A divine discontent is built into the energetic matrix of the soul, which provides the momentum for all that occurs on the journey back to the Creator. It is important to understand that the eternal soul is motivated by an ongoing desire to search for and find a higher level of expression.

Those who are not aware of the reason for this continuous expression of restless dissatisfaction cannot see the positive purpose it holds in the development of the soul. It provides a pulsation of vibratory energy that keeps the soul in a never-ending state of upward movement. Many who do not know the source of the discontent find themselves seeking release through a variety of addictive behavior patterns.

They think that continuous activity will provide a respite from their ongoing tension, when physical action is the opposite of what they need. They do not know that sitting in quiet attunement with one's soul essence will bring the relief they so desperately desire. Inner communication with one's higher self provides the knowledge and wisdom to ascertain what is for the highest good during each step of life's journey.

It is for this reason that we speak over and over again about the importance of regular meditation. Quiet inner attunement is the pathway to contact with the soul. When one is in continuous communication with the spiritual source of one's being, life opens up a vast field of consciousness that connects with the many dimensions of time and space. Humanity is on the threshold of the higher dimensions and is taking the first tentative steps to enter this new reality. We ask that you dare to trust and explore this new state of being.

Many ancient cultures considered it a sacred duty to record their story in song, in myth or in written form, which then was handed down to those not yet born. It was a very important task to keep alive the knowledge that had been acquired by their wisest elders throughout many lifetimes. The accomplishment of this task was based on the concept of linear time.

As the soul rises through the many dimensions of the Creator, it ascends from the simplest to the most complex, with each level forming the foundation required to move upward on the spiral of life. We wish to emphasize that each experience on the soul's journey is a valuable contribution to its overall advancement.

In a three-dimensional reality, time is segmented into compartments, which are not interchangeable in any way. In order to anchor the knowledge of time into the soul's consciousness, it was necessary to explore the triune nature of time. Each reality of past, present and future needed to be experienced thoroughly before the unity of time could be understood and embraced. The inhabitants of your planet have completed this task and are now ready to ascend into fourth-dimensional consciousness where the reality of time can now be seen in its entirety.

Time on the Fourth Dimension

There are many different dimensions within the universes of the Creator. The spiral is an accurate visual representation of the energetic matrix of a universe. Each circular movement within a spiral rises to a higher level than the one before it. As a soul ascends to the next level of the spiral, it carries with it all the knowledge it has gleaned from each former dimension.

Time with its triune makeup is experienced through the many human lifetimes of Earth's inhabitants. Those incarnating on your planet are now ready to move into the fourth dimension of time. In the fourth dimension, time is not compartmentalized into three different segments. All life unfolds within the Ever-Present Now.

By that we mean that every type of experience at the fourth dimensional level is occurring simultaneously. There is no past, present or future. Everything is occurring in the Now. For those living within the framework of the third dimension, this is a very difficult concept to grasp.

Perhaps it will help to think of a vast tapestry depicting many different scenes of great beauty. Each scene offers a unique picture of a complete story containing many different elements. If one could see the weaving in its entirety, the overall picture would become readily apparent to the viewer, each separate scene presenting an integral part of the whole. This analogy expresses the energetic blueprint for the fourth dimension.

There is no separate compartmentalization of past, present and future. What has happened in the past is really emerging in the present and includes within it elements of the future. The best way to experience this phenomenon is to become quiet, breathe deeply and connect with your inner soul essence.

Visualize some incident that has occurred in the past. See where it is connected to what is presently occurring. Then observe a possible future that contains elements of this past and present incident. Now go ever deeper within your consciousness and, through the power of mental intent, allow the three separate elements of time to merge and unite into one reality—the Now. If you are able to do so, you have started to experience the reality of the fourth dimension.

Another way to comprehend this new concept of time is to visualize you standing next to a river. Look both upstream and downstream until it disappears from sight. The view you have from this spot is all that you can see and know about the river. Now imagine yourself rising far above the river to where you can discern its source and its end. You are able to see it in its entirety. This complete picture of the river in its movement from start to finish presents an accurate representation of the concept of time in the fourth dimension.

Now, let us take one step further. As your understanding deepens, visualize what you have seen as the future returns to your combined past-present awareness and joins with it. Look at what you have created in your mind's eye. What supposedly happened in the past has become an integral part of what constitutes your present, which in turn will contribute to what unfolds in the future.

When you are able to see the triune nature of time as one complete and interconnected whole, you will have begun to experience a faint portion of fourth-dimensional reality. In order to do so, you must broaden the outer limits of your consciousness. It will be necessary to see yourself in a larger capacity—one that allows an expanded view of time to exist within your current mental framework.

If you are able to accomplish what we have presented here, you will have performed important preparations in expanding your awareness. Humanity on the Earth plane is beginning the ascent up the spiral of life to the next dimension. In order to do so, it must learn to "think outside the box," a current phrase used to describe the process of upgrading one's vision to include a broader view of reality. Open up the box of your third-dimensional plane and look out. There is a fascinating world waiting for you to enter and explore.

It is also vitally important that those incarnating on the Earth plane understand what is happening to change time as they know it. Divine energy emanating from the center of your universe is accelerating and causing life forms to oscillate in increasing waves of movement, which are breaking up rigidity and crystallization.

Because of this, all aspects of life seem to be moving at an ever-faster pace. The days appear to be getting shorter, and many complain that there aren't enough hours to accomplish all that needs to be done. Also, more and more people seem to be experiencing unexplained lapses of time, where they simply lose track of time and are surprised how fast the day has gone without their even being aware of it.

This change is partly explained by what we have said above. Universal energy waves are speeding up the construct of time during an evolutionary surge of soul growth. But the other half of the equation can be explained by the alteration that is occurring within the physical, emotional and psychological makeup of human beings incarnating on your planet. The molecular makeup of the body is being transformed at a deep and substantive level.

Bursts of spiritual energy waves radiating onto Earth are causing the electrical systems of human bodies to mutate and form new synapses and pathways in the brain. When a more advanced human species appears in the future, they will benefit from the increased brain capacity developed by those who came before them. They will be able to expand their manifesting capabilities far beyond what is possible today.

As it is now, the human brain functions in the range of fifteen percent of total capacity. In the centuries ahead, because of the constant vibratory impulses from the universal core, the human brain will increase to somewhere in the range of thirty-five to forty percent capacity. This expansion of the brain will bring about more advanced functioning in all areas of human life. Presently, the primary reflection of this development is within the experience of accelerated time.

The fourth dimension of time is the next step in the evolutionary journey of the soul, unifying past, present and future into the Eternal Now, where everything happens simultaneously. As the stimulus for evolutionary spiritual growth enters the Earth plane, divine order dictates that the next level above the third dimension will be the most impacted.

This is why everything connected to time is so greatly affected today. When a person grasps what is happening in this area of existence, the soul immediately responds with the deep intuitive knowing available to all. A sense of relaxation and trust floods the being, bringing about a release of anxiety and tension that is palpable. Then one can move into a co-creational relationship with Source, using time as a springboard into a higher spiritual realization.

CHAPTER 8

Multidimensional Consciousness

There is a core of humanity on your planet that is ready to move into multi-dimensional consciousness. Eons have elapsed since this journey began. Human beings on your planet have been preparing for this great shift for ages. Life on the three-dimensional plane had to be firmly anchored before any major step up the spiral of life could occur.

Many different cultures came into existence to present opportunities for spiritual growth and development. Each culture emphasized certain life experiences and lessons. The accumulation of what has been learned provides the foundation for entry into higher dimensions. To show specifically what we mean, we will take a moment to reflect with you on the primary themes of two cultures in the past.

As a first example, let us look at the Mesopotamian countries of the Fertile Crescent in the Near East. The people who lived in this area built great civilizations that emphasized writing, agriculture, building, commerce and trade, astronomy, religion, law, and specific forms of warfare. Many different human skills and abilities came into being and contributed to sophisticated advancement for those people that followed.

The Mayans of Central America also established a fixed societal format, which brought the stability needed to study the heavens and develop a system for recording vast stretches of time into the millions of years. Their discoveries focused on the galaxy, creating a springboard for advancements in space exploration and travel that will appear in the twenty-first century and beyond.

Each culture that has been in existence on Earth has contributed to the growing knowledge and skill base of humanity. Even the warlike, destructive civilizations have provided the experience of pain and suffering resulting from physical conflict. As souls have incarnated in a wide variety of different cultures, they have gained knowledge and wisdom regarding what it means to live on the third dimension of this universe.

Enough effort has been spent at this level. It is now time for incarnating souls on Earth to move up to the next dimension of experience—the fourth dimension of time. As more and more individuals take this momentous step, humanity as a whole will be uplifted and transformed. Human awareness will grow, as brain capacity increases to accommodate the influx of new information that will expand the neural pathways of the brain.

There is a burgeoning global interest in the spiritual dimension of life. More and more people are starting to believe in the multidimensional aspect of the human condition. The practice of meditation is taking many people deep within themselves, where they are encountering a presence transcending the outer physical world that has been their emphasis up to now.

There is a tangible feeling when they go within that is new for them. It is as if their world suddenly has expanded and deepened, moving them into a realm profoundly different from that which is familiar. Over time, their sensing and knowing capabilities are being broadened as they descend ever deeper into a peacefulness that can never be experienced in the outer world.

Those who meditate are moving into direct contact with the soul, which resides within each individual. This essence is a spark of the Creator and possesses eternal life. It is a basic unit of energy, which can never be destroyed. Understanding this, one knows that death impacts only the outer physical sheath and cannot destroy the spirit within. The realization that there is part of us that never dies, continually moving on through time, space and beyond, dramatically changes the view one has of life.

The fear of death diminishes and gradually disappears. As one begins to access one's inner soul wisdom more regularly, extrasensory capabilities begin to develop and expand. The soul has the ability to know what is happening elsewhere, or what is yet to come, without any factual information to confirm its reliability. This is one of the capabilities of the soul. The soul has a breadth of knowledge and wisdom that is far superior to human consciousness. Connecting with the soul makes extrasensory perception commonplace.

The soul can project its consciousness into many different realms of existence. When one fuses concrete three-dimensional awareness with the higher vibratory field of the soul, it is like being plugged into a more powerful energy circuit. One is able to see, hear and know much that the human brain cannot access. Connecting with the soul eventually allows an individual to experience other dimensions, where the lessons learned on the Earth plane provide a stepping stone to further spiritual growth and development.

The Interconnectedness of Time and Space

The people currently living on Earth are most fortunate in many ways. They have been selected to participate in an evolutionary step forward, which will transform the planet and all those living on it. This advancement also will raise the level of consciousness, making it possible to access other levels of existence.

All the dimensions of time and space are interconnected, and the wide varieties of life forms that live in them interact with each other. Therefore, a major shift or development occurring in one area of the universe will have a direct effect on life on other dimensional levels. This knowledge opens a doorway into higher spiritual awareness, impacting every incarnating soul on many different planes.

As the inhabitants of Earth go about their daily lives, there is little recognition that they are being constantly bombarded by energy from within their galaxy and beyond. As we have said before, the universes of the Creator are woven together like a huge tapestry with many different scenes. Together they offer a complete and harmonious picture of great beauty.

Not only is all of creation connected, but time itself is a reality far different from the current belief in the framework of past, present and future. Time is a continuous flow of the Ever-Present Now. There is no past or future as those on the three-dimensional plane think they experience it. Everything is unfolding simultaneously in a flowing interconnectedness that is glorious to behold.

Life is carried in a band of shimmering light that wafts through the farthest reaches of space, bringing a multiplicity of experiences to all of God's creation. One of the most significant advances for incarnating souls on Earth will be to recognize that they live in the vast energy field of the Almighty, reflecting the complex beauty of what has been created. When this primal truth is incorporated into conscious knowing, it will be a major accomplishment.

For many eons, human awareness has been anchored in dense three-dimensional realities. This phase of development has been a necessary part of God's plan for creation. Spiritualizing matter has always been the goal of existence on your planet. It is the cornerstone for the beautiful mosaic that constitutes life in the many realms of time and space. But now humanity is ready to move on.

Every evolutionary step involves a change in consciousness. Human beings are on a journey to become ever more complex in their basic essence. In order for this to happen, their molecular structure must be reconfigured so that they can absorb more powerful energy emanations, which will change them in many ways. Their physical bodies, and particularly their brain capacity, must be modified and expanded to hold the more advanced vibrational field that is coming into every facet of their being.

To illustrate this reality, we would like to address what occurs when one heals a traumatic situation in his or her life. Once a person is able to rise above a trauma that has been experienced and gains a higher state of awareness regarding it, light and love emanates out into the greater field, bringing healing to others who have struggled with the same issue but have not been able to overcome it.

This phenomenon is most easily understood as it manifests within a family dynamic. When an individual heals an area of trauma and suffering, all earlier generations of that person's family who struggled with the same issue receive healing through the achievement of the family member who conquered something they could not.

Let us look at a specific problem that often is repeated through a number of generations. The Bible spoke of this phenomenon when it said that the sins of the father are visited unto the son until the seventh generation. Behavioral patterns and their consequences surface over and over again, bringing the same challenge through the years to certain members within a family grouping.

Let us take, as an example, the recurrence of alcoholism within a certain family down through successive generations, causing pain and suffering in many ways to all those impacted by this devastating disease. When an alcoholic in a family acknowledges the problem, addresses the emotional, psychological and spiritual reasons for the addiction, and achieves healing, all previous alcoholics within the family are positively impacted at a soul level.

We know that this is a difficult concept to grasp when one looks at time in a linear framework. The concept of linear time was created to give the inhabitants of Earth a framework within which the Law of Cause and Effect could unfold. But when one experiences the fourth-dimensional reality of time, it all becomes very clear. On the fourth dimension, time is non-linear. All life is occurring simultaneously within the Eternal Now. There is no past, present and future. Everything is happening at the same time in a vast kaleidoscope of sound, color and movement.

Every segment of life exists within a unified field, and all souls are connected energetically within this field. When one individual overcomes an illness like alcoholism, all those who have struggled with the same issue are infused with healing energy, even though they were not able to cure themselves. In a fourth-dimensional reality, the individuals within these generations are all living at the same time and affecting everyone else at an energetic level.

There are two important elements to what we have said here. First, all of our actions impact life on many planes of existence, making it possible not only for a person to heal, but also to bring healing to many others. Secondly, incarnating souls on Earth are starting to experience the reality of the fourth dimension. Here the unity of time can be realized in its entirety by knowing with certainty that we can impact each other in this way. When this awareness is reached, the imperative to live lovingly and responsibly will become an integral part of our nature, raising us up to a higher level on the spiral of life.

An Expanded View of Self

It is our task to assist in preparing the inhabitants of your planet for the massive changes that will be occurring throughout this century and beyond. In order for a new phase of human evolution to begin, it is necessary to sweep away the aspects of life currently in existence that are no longer useful.

This process is well underway and has been for some time, extending back into the earliest days of the previous century. Much has been learned by those who have lived in the past on your planet; and much still must be experienced in order for humanity to achieve a higher form of expression. All life is ever evolving in a form of forward and upward movement.

Keep this idea fixed in your mind and continue to visualize this picture as the framework for all that you do. No matter where you are, you are always advancing on your spiritual path, even though it may seem to be just the opposite. The most negative and painful experiences are only grist for the mill, as the old saying goes, because your primary purpose is to immerse yourself in every aspect of God's world.

Your soul was brought into existence to attain a complete and comprehensive knowledge of what it means to live in the many universes of time and space. You provide an opening through which the Source of All That Is can actively participate in its own creation. And since your universe is predicated upon the principle of duality, you will experience the most positive and the most negative that life has to offer.

If you can accept this profound concept, you will be able to weather the storms and upheavals of life, knowing that you are here to grow in strength, understanding and love. In order for this to happen, the soul, like a pearl, is constantly worked and scraped until it ultimately becomes something beautiful to behold. The goal of the soul is to embrace whatever occurs in life with calm acceptance and loving equanimity.

The soul is always surrounded by many other souls of similar vibration. Each soul is part of ever-widening clusters of spiritual beings that extend out to the farthest reaches of creation. As the ability to see oneself within this more expanded framework grows, communication and interaction with one's soul group will increase, filling you with a profound sense of peace and joy, which will elevate all that you do and are.

One of the most significant developments of this current millennium will be the growing recognition by many that they possess an immortal soul encased in a physical body. The awareness of the role the soul plays in an individual life will come with this recognition. We cannot emphasize strongly enough how important this knowledge will be in the course of human evolution.

Just think about this concept for a moment. Many people on Earth during this twenty-first century address the various issues in their lives from the standpoint of the mundane impact these issues have upon them. They observe the physical reality of what they are facing and reflect intellectually and emotionally upon the various ramifications of these issues. Rarely do they go within and access their inner spiritual knowing during their decision-making process.

This is because they do not believe that they possess within themselves a deep, abiding spiritual wisdom. In fact, many incarnating souls on Earth's plane make decisions in an incomplete context that is limited in scope and effectiveness. This reality is in the process of major evolutionary change.

The divine Plan of the Creator has established a progression that unfolds in order and harmony. Every advance of humanity builds upon what has come before. This process resembles the unfolding of a beautiful flower, which proceeds in a measured cadence of growth towards its highest expression. Each step from a seed to a fully mature plant proceeds organically and in its own right time.

So it is with the spiritual journey of the soul. It started enclosed in the powerful vortex of the God Force, joined and at peace and harmony with the all-powerful center of the universe. Then individual units of consciousness were suddenly and forcefully expelled out into the unknown darkness of space to begin their long journey of exploration. Only when that journey has come to its conclusion will they merge back into total union with their Creator.

Do you or others you know look at your existence in this way? If you do, you are entering multidimensional consciousness, which provides an expanded view of self in every area of life. Each of you is an eternal soul with the qualities of the Creator at the core of your being. The expanded intelligence, wisdom and power of that Prime Source is easily and readily available at a moment's notice whenever needed. Draw upon it. It will sustain you in all that you do.

CHAPTER 9

The Journey Home

We would like to speak now about the significance of the books we have created with our receiver on the Earth plane. They are meant to connect and resonate with the heart energy in each person who reads our words. The beat of each human heart is calibrated to a cosmic frequency that pulsates throughout your universe.

This frequency has an underlying rhythm, which resonates beneath the surface of existence, galvanizing life at every level. It has been recognized by many advanced cultures on your planet and given a wide variety of names. In the Hindu tradition, it is called Shakti—the eternal cosmic pulsation that brings everything into being through the power of love.

On Earth, love has always been associated with the human heart. This idea is the basis for a more profound truth, existing at a cosmic level. The ancient saying "As above, so below" speaks to the close connection the heart has with the universal Shakti, which is the primary creative force in the universe.

The highest spiritual principles are reflected at ever-descending levels throughout time and space in a repetitive pattern that increases in density. Think of the beauty and order in what we have just said here. Every life form, no matter how varied or different, beats in harmony with the universal rhythms of the Creator in a divine symphony of magnificent proportions.

On the third-dimensional level, the human heart with its accompanying chakra is the receiver of the Shakti impulses. The heart's beat is calibrated to the exact rhythm emanating from the center of the universe. Through this connection, a cosmic synchronicity is established that never wavers. When an individual on Earth suffers a heart attack, one of the primary reasons is interference in the heart's capacity to absorb the universal energy coming from outer space.

This inability to receive can have a wide variety of causes, but the ultimate reason for the physical problem rests in the decrease of life force to the heart. This is why we continually speak about the importance of meditation and other yogic practices, since they assist greatly in balancing the human body to receive the universal energies constantly being beamed into it.

We do not want to diminish the physical, emotional or psychological reasons for heart problems since they are catalysts for the interruption and weakening in the flow of life force. The final physical condition exists, however, in the loss of the universal energy sustaining the heart. In the years ahead on your planet, the spiritual function of the heart will be recognized and honored.

We have spoken often of the need to feel gratitude and to celebrate the gift of life here on the Earth plane. We know that many have difficulty achieving this positive view when distressful conditions are surfacing everywhere. By seeing the ultimate good in all that transpires, however, an individual brings balance and harmony into every life situation.

The primary theme of your universe is, "We will resist what is opposite until we learn that we are all One." The Law of Duality forms the cornerstone for this theme, because only through experiencing polarity can the spiritual goal of unity be reached in all realities. The oneness of love and unity holds the highest spiritual vibration in the universe, since it contains at its core the divine love of the Creative Force.

It is important to see the existence of duality in every area of your life. Just a few examples of the opposites experienced in the human condition are: day and night, life and death, and love and hate. People find it difficult to accept the principle of duality and generally strive for whatever is best from their personal point of view.

When one experiences the opposite of what one wants, it is seen as something to be confronted and overcome. This view of life sets into motion a win-or-lose struggle, making unity impossible. Whenever differing positions are missing from the final outcome, an imbalance is created, preventing harmony.

The sense of victory gained over an opponent is actually a defeat at a higher spiritual level, since no common ground respecting the desires of both positions has been reached. By neutralizing competition, a new paradigm can emerge built on collaboration and cooperation, which then leads to the spiritual goal of unity.

We ask that you start to think in terms of what we have said here. Recognize that every life situation contains the seeds of its opposite. Honor the role of differences. Try to incorporate the existence of duality into your own frame of reference. Accept that it is necessary to achieve wholeness and the higher spiritual expression of unity.

Develop a conviction that striving for common ground and unity is preferable to confrontation and conflict. Make this belief a guiding light for you in every area of your life. When you have developed this inner resolve, you will become a messenger for peace and harmony— something sorely needed at this time on your planet.

Achieving Peace

On Earth, the drums of war beat loudly, drowning out the voices calling for peace and reconciliation. The forces of domination and control seem to be in the ascendancy, with warfare being trumpeted as the most effective way to solve a nation's problems. As more and more people come to understand that peace and unity are the ultimate goal for humanity, conflict and war will decrease, and a new day will dawn. Love and respect will become the guiding principles for humanity.

It is now necessary that a state of peace be achieved in the affairs of individuals, groups and nations. It has long been designated in the Plan of God that during this current period those on the Earth plane address this issue and master its spiritual dynamic. At its root, conflict of any type runs counter to basic spiritual principles.

The primary essence of the Creator is love. Every aspect of life in all the many dimensions contains the elements of the God Force. All human beings on your planet have at their core an eternal soul, which is a spark of this Force. Since the soul contains the spiritual qualities of its Creator, each soul has love as its fundamental guiding principle.

The Plan of the Creator has been to send particles from Source out into the many dimensions to experience every aspect of creation. In this way, the Creator will be able to know and enjoy the wide variety of what has been made in all its various forms. As a reflection of its source, each human being on this journey carries the spiritual imprint of love within the matrix of the soul.

When one acts counter to the love principle, it opposes the purpose for existence and sets up a spiritual dissonance that permeates the body, mind and emotions. This discord seeps into every aspect of the being. One falls out of balance and operates from a state of disharmony instead of from that which is the true nature of the soul.

As long as human beings do not know that they have a soul containing the qualities of the Creator, there will be no recognition of the spark of spirit impulsing every element of life. No congruence will exist between spirit at the core and the outer manifestation of physical existence. When one is in this state, there is no connection to the true purpose for being.

For this reason, one of the most vital tasks at the present time is that the people of Earth know and believe they are soul-infused. Once they recognize and own this truth about themselves, life takes on a totally different tone and hue. It will become essential to connect to and access the wisdom that resides at the core of the being. The practice of meditation, which provides a conduit to the inner self, will become a necessary part of life on a regular basis.

When the soul guides one's decisions, instead of the human personality, life is lived in a totally different manner. Every thought and act mirrors the elevated spiritual principles of the Source. It simply is not possible to have strife or conflict of any kind, because they run counter to the basic spiritual principles of love and respect. The recognition of the existence of the soul within, and this recognition alone, will provide the impetus for bringing about the end of warfare on your planet.

It is also of prime importance to understand the role the heart plays in the spiritual evolution of humanity. The heart receives the creative love energy from the center of the universe and transforms it into concrete, physical action on the three-dimensional level. When used in its highest form, it is an energy that brings about fusion and unity.

The people of Earth are living in a time of polarity and duality. Every area of life unfolding at the present time is doing so within this framework. One example can be found in the political arena. The vast majority of countries around the globe are experiencing political strife and discord caused because diametrically opposed factions seem to have equal strength and support.

Contrasting sides often go through a familiar pattern of hardening their stances and developing crystallized positions. Little progress can be achieved when two differing sides rigidly refuse to acknowledge any merit in the position of their opponent. At the present time, this pattern continually repeats itself in a wide variety of life situations.

It is for this reason that humanity all over the planet is grappling with the challenge of how to bring unity out of situations where polarity has become firmly entrenched. Whether this situation surfaces within interactions on a personal level, in the workplace, on the political scene or between nations, the underlying dynamic is still the same.

The heart energy of love has been blocked, making it extremely difficult to reach a satisfactory conclusion that both sides can agree upon and support. Intense polarity causes a reduction in the vibratory rate of an energy field and is sensed immediately on a soul level. Those with honed intuitive skills can identify the negative impact of any polarized set of circumstances. When conflict has reached a stalemate and resolution seems beyond reach, there will be a noticeable loss of energy.

To really appreciate the need for unity, one must experience the dissonance of duality. The love vibration of peace and harmony is the highest principle in the universes of the Creator. The soul's journey is made up of a multiplicity of experiences that will end when love is primary in the many dimensions of time, space and beyond. The task for incarnating souls on the Earth plane is to face the challenge of duality in all areas of life and bring about unity through intent, focused will and love.

Opening the Heart Chakra

The primary goal on the third dimensional level of Earth at the present time is to open the energy field surrounding the human heart, known as the heart chakra. In order to evolve, humanity must learn to live in a heart-directed way. For the past four hundred years, humanity's development has centered on increasing mental abilities. This period was necessary after centuries of a religious and faith-based approach to life. The left brain had to be developed, and now the focus has shifted to balancing the human persona.

This is to be accomplished by emphasizing the heart function, which in turn will bring the unifying power of love to the human condition. In order for this shift to occur, it will be necessary for incarnating souls on Earth to set aside anger, conflict and war. These emotional states create a dense and negative vibratory field wherever they are in evidence and shut down the love energy of the heart.

It is time for humanity to take responsibility for its actions. All life unfolds in a unified field, which affects everything contained within it. An act of anger does not exist in a vacuum. The intensity of its emotional vibration is propelled out into time and space, adversely affecting far more than one can imagine. And when anger is amplified within an act of war, the harm is increased one hundredfold.

Spiritual forces are being beamed from the center of your galaxy into your solar system, impacting Earth on a continuous basis. The vibratory message currently contained within these forces is a powerful one indeed. This spiritual directive is clear. Stop harming each other and the planet through acts of conflict and war. The primary manner in which this can be accomplished is through the introduction of the heart love energy.

Love is kind, supportive and refuses to do harm. Just think of how a conflicted situation would change if the individuals, groups or countries involved decided that they would do no harm. Political interaction between nations would be irrevocably changed if the principle of doing no harm were conscientiously followed. When positive support becomes a basic tenet for human interaction, the dynamics of conflict will be transformed.

Therefore, it is imperative that incarnating souls on Earth open their hearts and commit to creating a new type of human being, one who will always interact with love and respect. Two forces will make this change possible—the spiritual principles of intent and will. We ask that you enter every personal interaction with the intent to open your heart and invoke your personal will to do no harm and seek what is for the highest good.

Once these principles become ingrained on an individual level, they will spread out into the affairs of groups, nations and eventually the world. Each small step introducing love energy will ultimately result in the creation of a New World—one based on harmony and balance. This advanced state will take centuries to attain, but the first steps are meant to be taken now. You, as a soul currently living on the Earth plane, agreed before incarnating to commit to this task. So we say to you, it is now time to begin!

Moving into Higher Consciousness

Those of you on Earth at the present time are fortunate in many ways. You chose to be a part of the great shift in consciousness that is occurring on many different planes throughout your universe. Your soul's journey is taking place within the continuous in-breath and out-breath of the Creator. The path of involution and evolution is the primary energy dynamic of the universe.

Earth is currently experiencing involution, which exists during the long period of time when the power of spirit is descending into every form of life. The Divine Creator moves elements of its energy field outward in ever-widening concentric circles, infusing all life with spiritual essence. This is a brief description of involution—the process by which Source expels vibratory waves of creative mind force, causing many diverse forms of life to come into existence.

A primary element within this great spiritual outpouring is the intent of the Creator. Many types of life are formed just for the sheer joy of the act itself. Love and creation are the basic essence of the Primal Force. Since all that is brought into being contains the energy from which it sprung, love and creativity form the cornerstone of life throughout the many realms of time and space.

We ask that you quiet yourself, close your eyes and go within. Sink deeper, ever deeper, into that spark of infinite wisdom that resides within you. Ask that you may touch that innermost part of your true essence. Sit in stillness as the awareness of who you truly are begins to permeate your consciousness. See if you can begin to feel the faintest glimmer of creativity and love that was given you as your foundation for life.

If you can tap into that higher knowing, your life will start to shift in unimaginable ways. Think of difficult people and situations you are currently encountering in your life. Visualize yourself coming from a loving position as you attempt to find a more creative way to connect with them. Begin incorporating a sense of love for yourself as a fundamental starting point for any type of interaction.

The primary force in the universe is love. From this love comes the desire to create, in order to bring that love into a state of manifestation. A man and woman who love each other have a deep-seated desire to create something that reflects their love. If you contemplate what we have said here by viewing life around you, you will recognize that almost all acts originate out of a desire to create, whether they are performed alone or with another.

For this reason it is important to do a fearless inventory of yourself and your life. Are you finding joy and creativity in your life? Do you truly love yourself? Do you live a life that reflects that love? Can you love others with a divine detachment that never tries to possess? Are you able to do whatever work falls to you in your physical realm with a sense of serene satisfaction? Do you trust all that is unfolding in your world? If you are coming from a state of love, you are manifesting your true spiritual nature. You are living a soul-infused life, reflecting the primary essence of your Creator.

A Beautiful Time for Spiritual Growth

For many on the Earth plane, this is a time of shifting sands and uncertain futures. Every area of life is in a continuous state of flux. Long-held values and dependable outcomes appear to be slipping away, creating a deep sense of anxiety regarding the future. Life seems to flow in a chaotic stream, resulting in a corresponding loss of trust about how things will turn out.

What a beautiful time for growth and substantive change! When the affairs of humans are static, very little transformation can occur. Stagnation sets in throughout the human spectrum, and the need for security and perpetuation of the status quo becomes the primary motivating factor in life.

These times create a positive environment for the assimilation of certain spiritual principles. We do not want to imply that periods of quiet integration do not have value in the affairs of incarnating souls on your planet. But when the universal energy starts to move and flow, it is an indication that the time for a spiritual step forward has been reached.

Think of a strong wind that suddenly blows in from the sea, shifting the topography of the sandy shore. Without the wind, the beach would be a still and unchanging place. The erosion caused by the wind sculpts the land into other configurations, providing a new setting for habitation and play. Without the power of the wind, these variations in the land would never take place.

Spiritual energy is like the wind. When vibratory waves from the center of the universe are projected out into space, all life forms are affected in a direct and powerful way. The entire physical construct of life is altered, just as the dunes on the beach are changed by the force of the wind.

The best way to deal with present events is to acknowledge that one's immortal soul is the guiding force in life and is attuned to the Source from which it came. This Source is sending out specific energies needed for a period of spiritual growth, where stable aspects of life will be modified so that a new path can be taken.

Therefore, we ask that you not grieve for what is past and has moved away from your frame of reference. Do not think in terms of what has been lost. Instead have gratitude for what has been learned and feel a sense of anticipation for what is to come. The eternal constant of existence is change. See life as a kaleidoscope of ever-shifting colors and shapes, reflecting the essence of the Creator, within which the soul gains knowledge and wisdom on its return journey home.

We now have reached the end of this third cooperative effort between the Earth plane and the realm of spirit. This book has concentrated on a subject that is vital to the evolutionary progress of human beings on the third dimension. The people of Earth need to learn to connect with the spiritual understanding they hold within themselves at a soul level in order to go forward.

To accomplish this task, it first is necessary that each individual believe that an eternal spiritual soul resides at the core of every human being. Once that truth is acknowledged, the next step is the realization that each soul is ultimately connected to every other soul in existence throughout time, space and beyond—and ultimately to the Creative Force of the Universe.

Throughout this book, we have woven many skeins of information intended to open your minds and hearts to the true reality of life. We have described the origin of souls as sparks of the Creative Force. We have offered brief glimpses of the long journey throughout time, space and beyond that all souls have had to take. We have spoken of life situations facing Earth's humanity from the perspective of the soul, which is very different than the mundane approach toward matters in your world.

As we have said before, humanity on your planet is preparing to take a major evolutionary step forward. In order to do so, it is necessary to see oneself as a spiritual being living within a physical body, traveling through the many universes of the Creator to reflect back the beauty of creation. There are many planes existing above that of the third dimension. The soul is meant to experience them all. This is the ultimate purpose for which the soul was created.

The vast majority of people on Earth have forgotten their true origin and nature. Now is the time for this awareness to be reclaimed at a conscious level. A wide variety of life forms can be found on every dimensional plane. Interacting with them expands the soul and adds to the accumulation of experience and wisdom for which each soul was created.

Finally, we have conveyed the fundamental truth that the many universes of the Creator have an underlying energy field of love, which provides the vibrational support for all that exists. The soul can tap into this field on a continuous basis and bring a richness and abundance to all facets of life.

We now bring our third series of transmissions to a close. From the realm of spirit, we beam our love on waves of shimmering light. Own the divine essence that is the nature of your soul. Dance in a state of high well-being, confident in the knowledge that you always are loved and supported by the Creative Source of the Universe!

We love you all.

The Lightbringers

INDEX

Other books by Nancy Van Domelen and the Lightbringers

Dreaming a New World is Nancy Van Domelen's first book of transmissions from a group soul calling themselves the Lightbringers. They speak about the human experience—past, present and future. Issues like fear, love, death, relationships, sexuality, addictions, developing personal power and healing—to name a few—are explored from a spiritual perspective. The book presents physical, societal, and cultural changes that will occur in the next 30 years with profound insights on September 11th. Ongoing reference is made about the emergence of a new human species with those currently living on Earth serving as pioneers for this coming age.
$14.95
180 pages
ISBN 0-9716106-0-6

The Higher Dimensions—Our Next Home, the second book in this series, brings another powerful message from the Lightbringers. They speak about the condition of the Earth, how we can heal and restore planetary balance and why we are having natural disasters. The book explores the polarity between the United States and the Muslim World, the war in Iraq and how we can find unity through spiritualization of the human heart. We are told about humanity entering the fourth dimension of time and the expansion of human consciousness that will occur. The ultimate goal, the Lightbringers say, is to love ourselves and others while functioning within a larger spiritual context.
$14.95
168 pages
ISBN 0-9716106-1-4

*To purchase books online or to receive more information,
go to the Shining Mountain Publishing website:*

www.shiningmountain.net.